BE LIKE ROWAN

The Pursuit of Excellence

Jason R. Doll

Be Like Rowan: The Pursuit of Excellence
Written By Jason R. Doll
Copyright © 2020. 2024. All rights reserved.

The story, *Getting A Message to Garcia*, by Elbert Hubbard

Published in the United States of America
ISBN: 13: 978-1717484413
ISBN: 10: 1717484417

Self-Help / Personal Growth / Success

ACKNOWLEDGMENTS

I want to thank:

Amy, Mallory, Morgan,
Madison, and Matthew Doll,
Vic and Jeanne Doll,
Brian and Steven Doll,
Connie and Rodger Dickinson,
Jessie Bribiesca, Steve Symonds,
Walter Makori, Daniel Liberty,
and John Gakanga.

In memory of Ivan and Valeria Wieters.

Thank you each for your encouragement, love, and support!

Complacency is the

enemy of success.

It's a silent killer.

– Jason R. Doll

On February 22, 1899, in one hour, American publisher and writer Elbert Hubbard wrote a 1500-word essay titled "A Message to Garcia."

Over 100 years ago, a brief article was written in roughly an hour to fill an empty space in the March 1899 issue of a magazine which was otherwise ready for publication. This seemingly insignificant work about a soldier in the U.S. Army has since become one of the most published documents in the history of the printed world. "A Message To Garcia" has been translated into every major language on Earth.

In 1895, the little island nation of Cuba was desperately struggling to be freed from Spanish rule. The Spanish soldiers who occupied the island oppressed and brutalized the people. By 1897, the situation had deteriorated to the point that there was rioting in the streets of Havana between nationalists and Spanish soldiers. The United States had a strong interest in Cuba. President William McKinley dispatched the battleship Maine as a visible indicator of the United States' presence in the country.

On February 15, 1898, an explosion rocked the Havana harbor, sinking the U.S. battleship, Main. With the American people upset, McKinley sent an ultimatum to Spain to get out of Cuba.

By April, the United States was at war with Spain in what we now call the Spanish-American War. The plan to liberate Cuba involved an insurgency led by General Calixto Garcia. President McKinley desperately needed to send a message to General Garcia to secure his cooperation and ensure the successful liberation of Cuba. There were no means at the time to correspond quickly, so a messenger was needed to relay the plans to the insurgency. But Garcia was lost somewhere deep inside the nation's mountainous vastness. "Someone said to the President, 'There's a fellow by the name of Rowan will find Garcia for you, if anybody can.'" [i]

So, McKinley summoned forty-year-old United States Army 1st Lieutenant Andrew Rowan. Rowan was given an oil-skinned pouch containing a letter from President McKinley with no further direction other than to ensure that it made it into the hands of General Garcia as fast as possible.

In the story "A Message to Garcia," it is described how Rowan, under disguise, entered the enemy lines in, crossed the island without being detected. He not only succeeded in delivering a message to Garcia, but also secured secret information relative to existing military conditions in that region. The information was of such great value that it held the key bearing to a quick ending and success of the U.S. Army.

The only instruction Rowan received from his commanding officer was to gather supplies, link up with Cuban sympathizers in Jamaica, and then deliver a "message to Garcia." On April 24, 1898, Rowan disembarked from a small fishing boat onto Cuban shores and, three weeks later, emerged on the other side of the island having accomplished his mission.

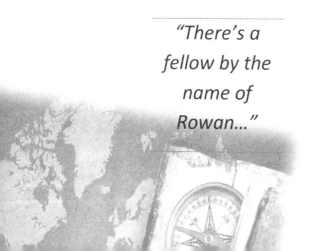

"There's a fellow by the name of Rowan..."

A MESSAGE TO GARCIA
by Elbert Hubbard
Originally published by the author in March 1899

In all this Cuban business there is one man stands out on the horizon of my memory like Mars at perihelion. When war broke out between Spain and the United States, it was very necessary to communicate quickly with the leader of the Insurgents. Garcia was somewhere in the mountain fastnesses of Cuba – no one knew where. No mail or telegraph could reach him. The President must secure his co–operation, and quickly.

What to do!

Someone said to the President, "There's a fellow by the name of Rowan will find Garcia for you, if anybody can."

Rowan was sent for and given a letter to be delivered to Garcia. How "the fellow by name of Rowan" took the letter, sealed it up in an oil–skin pouch, strapped it over his heart, in four days landed by night off the coast of Cuba from an open boat, disappeared into the jungle, and in three weeks came out on the other side of the island, having traversed a hostile country on foot, and having delivered his letter to Garcia, are things I have no special desire now to tell in detail.

The point I wish to make is this: McKinley gave Rowan a letter to be delivered to Garcia; Rowan took the letter and did not ask, "Where is he at?" By the Eternal! There is a man whose form should be cast in deathless bronze and the statue placed in every college in the land. It is not book–learning young men need, nor instruction about this or that, but a stiffening of the vertebrae which will cause them to be loyal to a trust, to act promptly, concentrate their energies; do the thing – "carry a message to Garcia!"

General Garcia is dead now, but there are other "Garcias" out there.

No man, who has endeavored to carry out an enterprise where many hands were needed but has been well–nigh appalled at times by the imbecility of the average man – the inability or unwillingness to concentrate on a thing and do it. Slipshod assistance, foolish inattention, dowdy indifference, and half–hearted work seem the rule; and no man succeeds, unless by hook or crook, or threat, he forces or bribes other men to assist him; or mayhap, God in His goodness performs a miracle, and sends him an Angel of Light for an assistant. You, reader, put this matter to a test: You are sitting now in your office – six clerks are within your call. Summon any one and make this request: "Please look in the encyclopedia and make a brief memorandum for me concerning the life of Corregio."

Will the clerk quietly say, "Yes, sir," and go do the task?

On your life, he will not. He will look at you out of a fishy eye, and ask one or more of the following questions:

Who was he?

Which encyclopedia?

Where is the encyclopedia?

Was I hired for that?

Don't you mean Bismarck?

What's the matter with Charlie doing it?

Is he dead?

Is there any hurry?

Shan't I bring you the book and let you look it up yourself?

What do you want to know for?

And I will lay you ten to one that after you have answered the questions, and explained how to find the information, and why you want it, the clerk will go off and get one of the other clerks to help him find Garcia – and then come back and tell you there is no such man. Of course, I may lose my bet, but according to the Law of Average, I will not.

Now if you are wise you will not bother to explain to your "assistant" that Corregio is indexed under the C's, not in the K's, but you will smile sweetly and say, "Never mind," and go look it up yourself.

And this incapacity for independent action, this moral stupidity, this infirmity of the will, this unwillingness to cheerfully catch hold and lift, are the things that put pure socialism so far into the future. If men will not act for themselves, what will they do when the benefit of their effort is for all? A first mate with knotted club seems necessary; and the dread of getting "the bounce" Saturday night holds many a worker in his place.

Advertise for a stenographer, and nine times out of ten who apply can neither spell nor punctuate – and do not think it necessary to.

Can such a one write a letter to Garcia?

"You see that bookkeeper," said the foreman to me in a large factory.

"Yes, what about him?"

"Well, he's a fine accountant, but if I'd send him to town on an errand, he might accomplish the errand all right, and, on the other hand, might stop at four saloons on the way, and when he got to Main Street, forget what he had been sent for."

Can such a man be entrusted to carry a message to Garcia?

We have recently been hearing much maudlin sympathy expressed for the "down–trodden denizen of the sweat shop" and the "homeless wanderer searching for honest employment," and with it all often go many hard words for the men in power.

Nothing is said about the employer who grows old before his time in a vain attempt to get frowsy ne'er–do–wells to do intelligent work; and his long patient striving with "help" that does nothing but loaf when his back is turned. In every store and factory there is a constant weeding–out process going on. The employer is constantly sending away "help" that have shown their incapacity to further the interests of the business, and others are being taken on. No matter how good times are, this sorting continues, only if times are hard and work is scarce, this sorting is done finer – but out and forever out, the incompetent and unworthy go. It is the survival of the fittest. self–interest prompts every employer to keep the best–those who can carry a message to Garcia.

I know one man of really brilliant parts who has not the ability to manage a business of his own, and yet who is absolutely worthless to anyone else, because he carries with him constantly the insane suspicion that his employer is oppressing, or intending to oppress, him. He cannot give orders, and he will not receive them. Should a message be given him to take to Garcia, his answer would probably be, "Take it yourself."

Tonight, this man walks the streets looking for work, the wind whistling through his threadbare coat. No one who knows him dare employ him, for he is a regular firebrand of discontent. He is impervious to reason, and the only thing that can impress him is the toe of a thick–soled No. 9 boot.

Of course I know that one so morally deformed is no less to be pitied than a physical cripple; but in your pitying, let us drop a tear, too, for the men who are striving to carry on a great enterprise, whose working hours are not limited by the whistle, and whose hair is fast turning white through the struggle to hold the line in dowdy indifference, slipshod imbecility, and the heartless ingratitude which, but for their enterprise, would be both hungry and homeless.

Have I put the matter too strongly? Possibly I have; but when all the world has gone a–slumming I wish to speak a word of sympathy for the man who succeeds – the man who, against great odds, has directed the efforts of others, and having succeeded, finds there's nothing in it: nothing but bare board and clothes.

I have carried a dinner–pail and worked for a day's wages, and I have also been an employer of labor, and I know there is something to be said on both sides. There is no excellence, per se, in poverty; rags are no recommendation; and all employers are not rapacious and high–handed, any more than all poor men are virtuous.

My heart goes out to the man who does his work when the "boss" is away, as well as when he is home. And the man who, when given a letter for Garcia, quietly takes the missive, without asking any idiotic questions, and with no lurking intention of chucking it into the nearest sewer, or of doing aught else but deliver it, never gets "laid off," nor has to go on strike for higher wages. Civilization is one long anxious search for just such individuals. Anything such a man asks will be granted; his kind is so rare that no employer can afford to let him go. He is wanted in every city, town, and village – in every office, shop, store, and factory. The world cries out for such; he is needed and needed badly – the man who can carry a message to Garcia.

Your challenge in life

is to become the

best possible version.

of yourself.

Not an imperfect approximation

of someone else.

– Jason R. Doll

Delivering A Message of Excellence

What amazes me about this brief essay is that its inspiring message still rings true today. The topic of this essay has become a symbol of various Nobel qualities every person longs for.

Lieutenant Rowan was the one person suggested to deliver the vital message to Garcia. This was no small task. He was given an assignment that seemed almost impractical and surly treacherous. Venturing somewhere into the mountains and through treacherous terrain and dangerous obstacles of a foreign land for nine days, Rowan and his team sneaking past the enemy, confronting a variety of dangers, all to find a man, hidden deep in the jungles. A man no one knew where he was. Rowan found him.

Immediately I asked myself, 'Why did they specifically choose Rowen to deliver this all–important message?'

Did their choosing Rowen have anything to do with things such as his rank, his age, his experience, his education, or his skills and knowledge?

The answer to this is simply: None of the above!

Rowan, a remarkable individual who has achieved tremendous success and made a profound impact, serves as an exemplary role model for those aspiring to greatness.

Rowan's journey teaches us valuable lessons about something critical and impactful that we can embrace in our own lives. The theme of Rowan and the principle behind the story are wrapped up in one word: *Excellence.*

Rowan was a person of excellence. His unwavering determination and mindset of excellence serve as a powerful example for us all.

Excellence is a quality that sets individuals apart, propelling them to achieve remarkable feats and surpass expectations. It goes beyond mere competence and embraces a relentless pursuit of greatness. Whether in personal or professional spheres, cultivating excellence can lead to fulfillment, success, and a lasting impact.

By exploring Rowan's story, we can gain valuable insights into how to overcome challenges, cultivate a mindset of excellence, and apply these principles to our own lives.

The world is in desperate need of people who embody excellence. People of excellence inspire others to aim higher, to break free from mediocrity, and to embrace their full potential. They set a positive example that spreads like wildfire, motivating others to pursue excellence in their own lives. People of excellence bring innovation, creativity, and problem-solving skills to the table. They have the power to make a significant impact and shape a better future for all.

In our fast-paced, interconnected world, the pursuit of excellence has become more important than ever. Mediocrity simply won't cut it anymore. Excellence sets us apart from the crowd and allows us to thrive amidst competition. It is the key to unlocking our full potential and achieving remarkable success.

Excellence. It's a word that carries weight and significance. But what exactly does it mean? At its core, excellence is about going above and beyond, exceeding expectations, and consistently delivering exceptional results. It's about striving for greatness in everything we do, whether it's our work, our relationships, or our personal pursuits. Excellence is not about being perfect, but rather about pushing ourselves to be the best version of ourselves.

Excellence is not a mystical quality reserved for a select few; it is a mindset and a set of attributes that we can all cultivate.

Excellence is a mindset, a commitment to giving your absolute best. It's about setting high standards for yourself and relentlessly pursuing them. It demands discipline, perseverance, and a willingness to go the extra mile. Excellence is not a singular act but a way of life. It is marked by a set of characteristics that define those who embody it.

Excellence is not just about being the best; it encompasses a mindset, a set of values, and a commitment to continuous growth and improvement. People of excellence possess the drive, skills, and determination to make a significant impact in their lives.

One of the key characteristics of excellence is a commitment to high standards. It means setting the bar high for ourselves and refusing to settle for mediocrity. Excellence requires us to consistently give our best effort. It's about raising the standard and not cutting corners, even when faced with challenges or tight deadlines.

Excellence involves challenging the norm and being willing to face tasks that others may shy away from. It entails persevering in the face of adversity to accomplish our goals.

Excellence is not a destination that we ultimately reach, but rather an ongoing process of continuous growth to become the best version of ourselves. It's a mindset. It's a lifestyle. It is a specific way of thinking and part of your makeup.

While each person's journey is unique, the principles and traits that define excellence are accessible to anyone. By learning from Rowan's example, setting goals, cultivating key habits, and embracing a growth mindset, you can strive for your own version of excellence.

One of the defining traits of Rowan's excellence is his unwavering perseverance and dedication. He understood that success does not come easily. Rowan's ability to stay focused and committed, even in the face of challenges, is a true testament to his character.

First and foremost, excellence is a mindset. Excellence requires a high level of commitment, discipline, and a refusal to settle for mediocrity. It's about embracing challenges, taking risks, and having the determination to overcome obstacles.

Lt. Rowan's selection for the world-altering task was based on his personal excellence. His unwavering perseverance and unwavering drive showcased his exceptional mindset. Perseverance is the unwavering determination to keep going, no matter the challenges or setbacks. It's the refusal to give up when faced with adversity.

Lt. Rowan's reputation for being dependable and surpassing mediocrity made him the ideal candidate for this mission. Personal excellence entails consistently performing ordinary tasks extraordinarily well. It is not merely meeting standards but rather setting them.

Lt. Rowan exemplifies personal excellence. When he accepted the mission, he did not receive a detailed checklist or a list of required supplies. He did not waste time organizing meetings or compiling questions. He did not seek the assistance of numerous experts or devise complex strategies. He did not inquire about alternatives or contingency plans. His objective was simple: deliver the message to Garcia. Lt. Rowan had one mission, one objective, and one priority.

The path to excellence is not without its challenges. It is important to note that there were no GPS devices, cell phones, Google Earth maps, internet access, text messages, or any means of knowing Garcia's location. Upon arriving in Cuba, Lt. Rowan embarked on an arduous eight-day horseback journey through the treacherous Sierra Maestra Mountains to locate and meet with Garcia.

Here's the thing: Once Rowan understood the task and he immediately set out to do what he was asked to do.

What sets Lt. Rowan apart is his immediate action upon understanding the task. He made no excuses and wasted no time. He went above and beyond the call of duty, refusing to give in to the numerous temptations along the way. Lt. Rowan formulated a plan and made a deliberate decision. He simply accepted the assignment and carried it out. Despite facing obstacles, Lt. Rowan persevered and successfully accomplished his mission.

What relevance does this hold in our contemporary society? How does this relate to your personal life?

In the present era, our ability to promptly respond to obligations, basic inquiries, fulfill commitments, and even carry out work duties is diminishing. We are reluctant to engage in anything that disrupts our daily routines, leisure time, social media activities, and virtual interactions.

Excellence is a virtue that has been revered and sought after throughout human history. It is the relentless pursuit of exceptional outcomes, the commitment to exceeding expectations, and the drive to continuously improve. In a world filled with mediocrity, achieving and maintaining a level of excellence sets individuals, organizations, and societies apart.

In a world filled with mediocrity and half-hearted efforts, excellence stands out like a beacon of hope. It's that magical quality that separates the ordinary from the extraordinary, the satisfactory from the outstanding. But what exactly does it mean to achieve excellence?

Today, our ever-evolving world is in desperate need of individuals who approach their tasks with unwavering dedication and excellence. Employers seek individuals who proactively seek solutions and take initiative, rather than relying on constant guidance. Organizations thrive when their members are willing to explore uncharted territories and create something extraordinary. Companies benefit greatly from individuals who are willing to step out of their comfort zones and give their utmost effort to achieve success.

Our world needs people who can be counted on at all times, and efficiently complete missions with minimal supervision – especially when the curtains are pulled back to find the most complicated moments.

Lieutenant Rowan exhibited and demonstrated a level of personal excellence. Rowan embarked on his mission without asking the President any details. He just did it. He simply took action and ensured its success. Once he comprehended the objective and its rationale, he pursued it with unwavering determination. He overcame any obstacles that came his way and remained fully committed to accomplishing his assigned task until the very end.

Rowan exemplifies a rare individual who is unwaveringly committed to accomplishing their task, regardless of what it takes. Are you prepared to do the same? Will you liberate yourself from the constraints of mediocrity and embrace a challenge to excel? Are you ready to offer an unparalleled standard of excellence? Will you pledge to elevate your personal excellence to new heights?

Executing tasks with a level of excellence is a more precious attribute than an educational degree or talent due to its shortage. Rowan promptly embarked on fulfilling his assigned duties, and he successfully accomplished them. He refrained from making excuses or delaying the process. He didn't require someone to provide him with elaborate instructions on how to complete the task. He didn't hesitate nor waste any time. Despite facing numerous temptations to quit, he persevered. His determination remained unwavering as he remained focused on his objective.

I see so many people searching and struggling to find greatness. They keep doing the same things the same way.

They walk the same path, often by rote, only to end up in the same place they started.

Do you long to hear your name called when time is short, and the stakes are high? Do you want others to know you are a person who can be trusted with important tasks on an important mission?

I can guarantee your employer will not call on you if you are not providing a quality and characteristic that sets you apart from others in your organization. To be recognized, there must be something different about you. Something that sets you apart. Good cannot be good enough. You must possess the discipline to aim for something greater. It necessitates a deliberate effort to strive for improvement. Following the same path as everyone else will not lead you to success.

Too many individuals resemble the six clerks that Hubbert mentioned in his story. If your supervisor were to request you to research and provide details about Correggio, how would you respond? If you were the supervisor, what would your employees say if you posed the same question to them? It is highly likely that they would bombard you with similar inquiries as the six clerks did... "Why do you need this information? Is it truly important that I need to do it now? I don't recall this being part of my job description. Can I do it next Monday? Can't Frank handle it?" This type of individual is not someone an employer can rely on.

When I request my department directors to identify the most suitable candidate for a specific position, they are already aware of whom they will ask to do the job. They are familiar with who the best person is to go above and beyond. They know who the individuals who are that are eager to take on the responsibility, demonstrate their utmost dedication, and possess a proactive 'can do' mindset. They bring me the individual who can be relied upon to fulfill the job requirements, take responsibility for their actions, and consistently perform at their best. The supervisor recommends someone who does not require constant supervision to stay on track, nor detailed instructions on how to accomplish tasks. Additionally, this person must possess the discernment to know when it is appropriate to seek clarification. My leadership team only presents individuals who consistently rise above the rest. They understand that I am seeking someone who can effectively deliver the messages.

Not only do I expect excellence from my employees, but I also strive to demonstrate personal excellence in all I do. I want to be on fire and full of zeal – driven with unwavering enthusiasm.

Many individuals hold the misconception that their most significant challenges will arise from unexpected occurrences and external factors. However, this is untrue. The greatest challenges come from within.

Woody Allen said that 90% of life is "just showing up." If so, then 10% of life is execution. Far too many people fail at doing either consistently. If the ability to execute is so valuable, why is it so rare?

You need to be different. Determine what makes you unique. What gets you on fire? What makes you stand out? What distinguishes you from the crowd?

Discovering your distinctive qualities and strengths will enable you to distinguish yourself from others. By cultivating a high level of personal excellence, you will establish a trustworthy reputation, making you the go-to person for significant responsibilities. As a result, you will find yourself in the spotlight, being sought after by those who recognize and sought after. You will be one who will be called on you to get a message to Garcia.

ARE YOU A ROWAN?

The point of this story I hope you will embrace is that no one knew where General Garcia was, yet Lieutenant Rowan promptly stepped forward to undertake the arduous journey across the Gulf of Mexico, vast stretches of dense jungle, and into enemy-held territory in order to obtain assistance from the resistance. He did not question, "Why should it be me? Why not another individual? Where can General Garcia be found?" Nor did he resort to the frequently given response of "That's not my job."

So, let me ask this question: If not you, then who? If it isn't you who rises up and goes forward, then who will? If you are asked to take the letter to Garcia, will you be a Lt. Rowan?

> The quality of our lives is directly proportional to our commitment level of excellence.

When given a task, do you rise and give your utmost effort? Are you willing to persevere despite obstacles and continue moving forward to deliver? Are you willing to surpass expectations? Are you one of the exceptional individuals who can successfully complete a difficult mission? Are you one of the rare individuals that can take a message to Garcia?

Or are you one of the other officers who were never even considered? There were many officers who could have been chosen, but they were not. Why? Because they were not like Rowan. And all around you, there are men and women who could be asked but because they are not committed to a level of excellence, they never are.

Can you remember giving a task to one of your employees and without bombarding you with numerous questions about the details?

How long has it been since your supervisor gave you an assignment and you gave more than asked? When did you last volunteer to take on a hard task?

Are you the kind of person whom others would rely on to successfully deliver a message to Garcia?

Each and every one of us has a person similar to a "Garcia" in our life in which we are called to seek and reach. My questions to you is this: Do you pursue personal excellence in your life? Have you made a commitment to pursue personal excellence? Are you prepared to emulate Rowan's determination? Are you prepared to do whatever it takes to achieve your goals? Are you ready to exert yourself in the pursuit of excellence?

The world is overpopulated and abundant with individuals who merely speak about their intentions but fail to take action. It is replete with individuals who procrastinate, display laziness, and prefer to remain within their comfort zones. Discovering individuals who are willing to progress despite challenges is a rarity. Our society expects exceptional performance, yet only a few are willing to deliver.

Unfortunately, a significant number of individuals in our vicinity lack the drive for excellence. They fail to exert additional effort or go beyond what is expected of them. Instead, they are preoccupied with counting down how much longer until they leave. They are too caught up in the things that don't' matter. They envelop themselves in a multitude of excuses, citing reasons why they cannot achieve, how occupied they are, or how life is unjust. Typically, these individuals incessantly complain about 'difficulties', all the while engaging in gossip and criticism, questioning why others have attained certain goals.

Do not underestimate the importance of this fact – you have a choice. Excellence is never an accident; it is always a deliberate decision. Personal excellence is an investment. It is our mindset that mirrors our enthusiasm and dedication. Personal greatness is optimizing your natural abilities, talents, and skills to perform at your utmost capacity. It is the outcome of caring deeply about your endeavors and exerting your utmost effort. It is an outward expression of inner integrity, desire, and a strong sense to make a true difference. It is about realizing your full potential, striving to be the best version of yourself, and cultivating a low tolerance for mediocrity.

The term "excellence" refers to the consistent display of good character, attitude, quality, and standards. It is not being satisfied with average. It entails surpassing mediocrity and focusing on meticulous attention to detail, thereby distinguishing oneself in any given situation. Moreover, it involves positively impacting the lives of others, not for the purpose of impressing them, but to leave a lasting impression. Being a person of excellence is an ongoing journey towards personal growth and development.

To embark on a journey towards personal excellence, it is crucial to grasp the true meaning of what excellence is. While the notion of striving for personal excellence may seem cliché, it is imperative to reflect and contemplate what excellence truly means to us. Therefore, it is essential to invest some time in refining our understanding and establishing a solid foundation for excellence.

Excellence is the essence of surpassing expectations, of wholeheartedly dedicating oneself to achieving the utmost in a particular endeavor. Excellence is characterized as the pinnacle of distinction.

Webster Dictionary defines excellence as "the state, quality or condition of excelling, superiority. Something in which one excels."

Excellent describes an action; but *Excellence* describes your core being.
Excellent (adjective) extremely good; outstanding.
Excellence (noun) the quality of being outstanding.

Certainly, the concept of excellence is frequently synonymous with words like *superior, best, success,* or *perfect.* However, *excellence* is not connected to any of those words. It is, in fact, an attitude and a character trait that demands concentration, passion, and dedication, where one is always prepared to offer their utmost.

Excellence is not a random occurrence or some accident we stumble upon. Rather it is a conscious choice that we must make. It is not something we are inherently born with, but rather something we develop through dedication and effort. Excellence is achieved by surpassing the established standards and expectations. It should be the guiding principle and defining characteristic of our lives.

The story of Rowan is more than him finding Garcia in the midst of what appeared to be an impossible situation. Like I first discussed, the question most people miss and don't ask is, why was Rowan was picked for this mission in the first place? Why was it Rowan and not someone else? What set him apart? It started years before the Spanish–American war.

Lt. Rowan was selected due to his unwavering commitment to being a reliable and resolute individual. With his name recommended to the President, Lt. Rowan was bestowed with the highest praise, "If anybody can find Garcia, it's Rowan."

Excellence is often associated with greatness and outstanding achievement. It is a quality that sets individuals apart and distinguishes them from the rest. In essence, excellence is about consistently exceeding expectations and delivering the highest possible standards in everything we do. Excellence is not a destination; it is a journey of continuous personal growth.

The journey of excellence is not solely about the destination but also the process itself. By immersing ourselves in the pursuit of excellence, we find meaning and satisfaction in every step of the journey.

Most people desire to be entrusted with significant tasks, yet they lack the willingness to put in the necessary effort. The pursuit of excellence is within the reach of all, but only a select few actually strive for it. Opting for excellence is a conscious decision. It entails undertaking tasks that the majority of individuals either cannot or will not undertake. Most people lack the determination to endure hardships. They are content with simply completing their duties and leaving as soon as their shift ends. At work, they are quick to leave when their shift is over. Their primary concern is whether they will receive a higher salary rather than if they can do better. They shy away from competition. Consequently, they are never entrusted with important assignments. They will never understand what excellence really is.

Excellence requires focus and total commitment. This level of distinction is attainable only by a select few individuals who possess the few people who are willing to take the risk and make the sacrifices necessary to stand out from the crowd. A very small percentage of people will try to achieve personal excellence, and even fewer number will wholeheartedly commit to a lifelong journey of unwavering devotion, even in the face of adversity.

Personal excellence is not a destination that one reaches on a bright and sunny day after years of relentless effort. Rather, it is a way of life that encompasses every aspect of one's existence. Embracing excellence means embracing our utmost potential and living accordingly. To live with excellence is to live our highest potential.

Many times, we focus primarily on *doing* and neglect *being*. What people often miss is that doing is rooted in being! While the seed of virtue undeniably resides within you, you must fan it to flame it. The keys to unlocking personal excellence is the will to push forward, the desire to succeed, and the urge to reach one's full potential. It represents a personal gauge for striving towards the highest levels of excellence and surpassing our own expectations - to become the best version of ourselves.

Being average is easy. It requires no effort, no ambition, and no desire for personal growth. But is that really the kind of person you want to be? Embracing a mindset of excellence means striving for greatness, pushing yourself to be better, and refusing to settle for mediocrity.

A mindset of excellence is all about aiming higher, pushing yourself to reach your full potential, and constantly seeking to improve. It's not about being perfect, but rather about embracing a continuous journey of growth and development. By adopting this mindset, you become dedicated to constantly being the best version of yourself.

The pursuit of excellence starts with one's mindset. It's a contest between what you've done and what you're capable of doing. Those who pursue their highest standards aren't in direct competition with others, they measure themselves against their own accomplishments. The principle of excellence lies in the pursuit of self-improvement.

Your toughest opponent isn't out there! It is inside you. It resides within you. Instead of contending with others, you must strive to surpass and confront your own future self.

Jack Nicklaus, the renowned golfer, understood this principle. He achieved success by directing his attention towards his personal achievements rather than dwelling on whether he was better than his opponents. In essence, he competed against the golf course, not his competitors. While others were pitted against Jack, he challenged himself. Jack came to the realization that reaching our utmost potential and surpassing our own expectations involves mastering our unique talents, abilities, and gifts.

Similarly, it holds great importance to perceive excellence not as an external benchmark, but rather as an individual gauge to measure our own accomplishments. A personal barometer for performance against our own standards. It serves as a motivation to refine ourselves and strive for a superior level of achievement. Your challenge in life is to become the best possible version of you. Not an imperfect approximation of someone else.

We need to exercise caution in not conflating success and excellence under the same category. Although they are frequently intertwined, they are two different things. Most people focus on success instead of excellence. We see success everywhere and it looks shiny and happy. It is displayed as effortless and seductive, like a well composed shot on a cover of a glossy magazine.

Excellence is not a destination; it is a journey of continuous personal growth. Those who excel understand the importance of learning, self-reflection, and self-improvement. They actively seek opportunities to expand their knowledge, skills, and perspectives, enabling them to adapt and thrive in ever-changing environments.

Cultivating a growth mindset involves embracing challenges, viewing failures as opportunities for learning, and believing in the power of effort and persistence.

Achieving personal excellence requires unwavering determination and steadfast dedication. You cannot buy it, hold it, and you can't cheat your way to it. True personal excellence cannot be attained by remaining within the confines of mediocrity.

Our modern society is facing a significant challenge that poses a threat to our way of life. The concept of 'good' has been overshadowed by the notion of 'good enough', which serves as a means to rationalize mediocrity. Regrettably, our world has embraced this mindset, becoming accustomed to settling for less. Sadly, our world has drunk enough of the poison, it has become accustomed to mediocrity. If you drink enough bad coffee, you'll gradually get used to it.

Mediocrity can be described as being "of moderate or low quality, value, ability, or performance." It signifies the state of being just average. Mediocrity is characterized by the reluctance to pursue personal growth and improvement.

Excellence is not just about being good at something; it's about going above and beyond, surpassing expectations, and continuously striving for improvement. Mediocrity, on the other hand, is the comfortable space where people settle for average. It's the acceptance of subpar performance and the lack of motivation to reach one's full potential. It's about doing the bare minimum and being satisfied with mediocre results.

People of mediocrity often lack ambition and drive. They are content with staying within their comfort zones and rarely push themselves to achieve more. They lack the motivation to set ambitious goals and take proactive steps to pursue them.

Mediocre individuals set low standards for themselves and often lack accountability for their actions. They may prioritize shortcuts, cutting corners, or delivering subpar work, which ultimately hinders their progress and limits their success.

When considering this term "mediocrity" in relation to my own life, it is completely contrary to the person I aspire to become and the impact I am determined to create.

There is a keyword in what I just said - commitment. Achieving even the simplest of goals requires us to learn the meaning of commitment. One must either be dedicated to attaining personal excellence or settle for a life of mediocrity. By settling, we settle for something inferior to our utmost potential. However, when we make a commitment to surpass mediocrity, we convey our anticipation for greater accomplishments, demonstrate our willingness to invest in self-improvement, and reject the status quo.

The key factor that distinguishes the minority who achieve greatness from the majority who remain average is their readiness to surpass their own limitations and fully utilize their capabilities by stepping outside their comfort zone.

A person of excellence experiences a greater sense of personal satisfaction and fulfillment. By constantly striving for excellence, they can see the progress they make and feel a deep sense of accomplishment. This fulfillment positively impacts their overall well-being and happiness.

Achieving excellence necessitates a willingness to invest the necessary effort to avoid shortcuts. Too many people try to find the shortcuts, the fast-track, and the easy way. A person of excellence is not like that. Lt. Rowan was committed and dedicated to achieving his best and refused to fail.

Being a person of excellence is the realization that it is better to do small things well than do big things poorly. Excellence is attained if you believe more than others, take the risks you need, and expect more than others think is possible.

Excellence is a concept that transcends mere competence and proficiency. It represents the relentless pursuit of the highest standards, the constant drive to improve, and the unwavering commitment to deliver quality in every endeavor. Whether it's in our personal lives or professional endeavors, striving for excellence enables us to reach our full potential and make a lasting impact.

To clarify my point, I want to emphasize that Excellence is an intentional way of living. Excellence is not an act, but a habit. It is not merely an isolated action, but rather a consistent practice. This quality sets apart extraordinary individuals from the average ones. It is important to note that excellence is not innate; rather, it is developed through continuous effort and dedication. Therefore, personal excellence is a deliberate way of living.

Excellence is not an aptitude; it is an attitude. It is the ability to continually deliver superior efforts with a positive mindset in everything you do. Personal excellence is not a fixed goal; rather, it involves an ongoing process of becoming the best version of oneself. It is holding yourself responsible for a higher standard than anybody else expects of you.

Personal excellence can be developed, but it is developed inborn. It resides within you, akin to a precious pearl nestled within a clamshell. Every individual possesses this pearl from birth; it simply requires a willingness to unveil it.

This is applicable to everyone, regardless of their occupation, whether they are a bus driver, police officer, custodian, teacher, pastor, truck driver, chef, CEO, hotdog vendor, or even the President.

Excellence entails maintaining a level of performance that surpasses the expectations set by others. It goes beyond merely meeting the minimum requirements; it involves establishing a new standard. It is about exceeding the status quo. A key to excellence is to consistently surpass the norm. Excellence is always asking, *"how can I do this better?"* or *"how can I do this to the best of my ability?"* A key to excellence is to consistently surpass the norm. Excellence is always asking, *"how can I do this better?"* or *"how can I do this to the best of my ability?"*

Excellence is not an occasional act that we perform only when we are aware of our boss or someone else observing us; rather, it is an inherent part of our identity, embedded in who we are, firmly ingrained within us.

There are multiple ways to achieve success. However, to reach one's greatest potential, it must be built on a bedrock commitment to excellence, and a rejection of mediocrity.

You have been designed to be distinguished. It is part of your makeup. This knowledge is evident because the One who brought you into existence crafted you as His ultimate creation. As stated in Ephesians 2:10, "For we are God's masterpiece. He has created us anew in Christ Jesus, so we can do the good things he planned for us long ago."

God's intention for you is not to blend in or settle for mediocrity. Instead, you have been summoned to rise above the ordinary and showcase excellence. Embrace your unique identity and strive to stand out among the masses. You are called to stand out in the crowd - to be a person of excellence.

In a world where mediocrity often seems to be the norm, individuals often seek shortcuts and settle for mediocrity as the norm, it is imperative that you resist conforming to the standards set by others. The manner in which you approach one task reflects your approach to all aspects of life. It is high time to elevate your actions and surpass the ordinary. Henceforth, refrain from taking any shortcuts or compromising on quality.

The key to leading a life of excellence begins with one's mindset and attitude. There is nothing as powerful as your mindset. It's a matter of programming your mind to think differently. It is about training your mind to adopt a different perspective.

> Excellence and mediocrity are not bedfellows – they never coexist.

Your current mindset shapes your outlook, both presently and in the days to come. Those who lack determination often find themselves trapped by their own actions.

Excellence is a mindset that permeates every facet of life. Your attitude colors every element of your existence. It resembles a brush wielded by the mind, capable of painting a vivid and captivating picture. Alternatively, it can scatter gloom and desolation, transforming the canvas into a futile portrait.

What is going on in your mind has such a huge impact on the actions that you take, on the decisions you make, and the things that you experience. You alter your mindset to focus on excellence.

The bottom line is: What you focus on is what you will reproduce. Your thoughts manifest into reality. You could say your beliefs are fruit producing.

Striving for excellence means setting high standards, challenging ourselves, and continuously improving. It's about embracing the mindset that good enough is never good enough because we know we can do better. It's about refusing to settle for mediocrity and embracing the idea that we are capable of greatness.

Dr. Martin Luther King Jr. once said: "If a man is called to be a street sweeper, he should sweep streets even as Michelangelo painted, or Beethoven composed music, or Shakespeare wrote poetry. He should sweep streets so well that all the hosts of heaven and earth will pause to say, 'Here lived a great street sweeper who did his job well.'"

Research has indicated that approximately 80% of individuals fall short of their own expectations. Another 15-18% managed to meet expectations but didn't surpass them. Consequently, a mere 2% of the global population consistently strive for intentionally elevated standards. This select group of individuals experiences the utmost satisfaction and successfully attains their life's passions and purpose.

What category do you currently belong to? Are you part of the 2% group? This group is characterized by individuals who always strive to give their best and aim for greater things. Alternatively, are you among the majority, the 97% who consciously choose not to surpass their current mental limits because they prefer to settle for what is safe and readily available? The good news is that it is doesn't matter which category you currently find yourself in; what truly matters is which one you aspire to be a part of.

How do we live a life that begins to exceed expectations? We *choose*. We should always expect more from ourselves than others expect from us. By opting to belong to the mere 2% who live above average, we must consistently strive to exceed the expectations placed upon us by others and set higher standards for ourselves.

Excellence and mediocrity are not bedfellows - they never coexist. When you actively choose to strive for excellence, you inevitably draw towards something of greater significance.

Embracing excellence is a choice that opens doors to personal and professional fulfillment. By refusing to settle for mediocrity, you give yourself the opportunity to explore your full potential and create a life that is meaningful and rewarding.

Thus, to better understand personal excellence there are different attributes of it which includes:

1. Self-Awareness
2. Commitment
3. Focus
4. Discipline
5. Courage
6. Passion
7. Vision
8. Attitude
9. Adaptability
10. Accountability
11. Growth Mindset
12. Calmness Under Pressure
13. Intentional Living
14. Encouraging and Motivated

Producing our best self isn't something that we do occasionally. It is not attained with a one-time, quick, and isolated tactic. It is a continuous, ongoing decision and action. It should be rooted deep within you as an intentional way of living - woven into the fabric of your life. You must be willing to do what other people are not.

Are you prepared to do whatever is necessary? Are you determined to rise above mediocrity and the status quo?

What do you typically observe when you look around at the majority of your colleagues, acquaintances, and relatives? What do you see in their habits, work and life?

I know what I see. A sense of complacency prevails among them. They seem satisfied with maintaining a level of safety within their comfort zone. They do not excel beyond the norm. They possess a mentality of "that's not my job" and are hesitant to go beyond their assigned tasks. Frequently, they arrive late, leave early, and rarely put in more effort than their colleagues. However, they are often quick to voice complaints about their life circumstances and lament the fact that they are never chosen for more significant opportunities.

Believe it or not, you can stand out simply by doing a few simple things that many other people won't do consistently. By developing a standard of these characteristics below, just like Rowan, you will be selected to do prodigious things.

To achieve personal excellence, it's important to identify the key skills and competencies needed in your chosen field. These could be technical skills, communication skills, leadership skills, or creativity, among others. Understanding the skills required will allow you to focus your efforts on developing and honing them.

You can go from good to great. It is all about developing a caliber mindset in everything you do and who you are.

Excellence is not just a word; it's a way of approaching life. It is the pursuit of greatness, the commitment to surpassing expectations and achieving remarkable outcomes. Having a clear vision is like having a roadmap to excellence. It's essential to identify what you want to achieve and where you want to go.

If you want to be like Rowan, you need to:

Define your priorities.
Be a visionary.
Have a plan.
Never quit.
Don't be afraid to fail.
Have high standards.
Be adaptable.
Make time - especially if you don't have it.
Be prepared to sacrifice.
Stay focused.
Stay positive.
Deliver your greatest commitment.
Be a person of valor!
Work hard, especially when no one is looking.
Set your goals into motion.
Put quality over quantity.
Believe you can.
Jump in with both feet!

By understanding and implementing these keys to excellence, you can unlock your full potential and strive for greatness in all that you do.

Most individuals tend to adhere to societal expectations and simply do what is required of them. They are content with leading an 'ordinary' life within the confines of their comfort zone, and they function to uphold the routine standards of work and personal life. However, individuals who hold themselves to higher standards do not and cannot conform to this norm. They possess a distinct mindset and approach to life. It is a deliberate way of living.

The real question is not, "Why should one pursue excellence?" but rather, "What motivates an individual to relentlessly pursue a higher level of personal excellence?"

The trap of mediocrity has trapped most people in their life. Are you familiar with the tale of the frog and the boiling water? According to the theory, if a frog is placed in a pot of boiling water, it will instinctively leap out to save itself. This parallels our survival instinct. However, if the frog is placed in lukewarm water and the temperature is gradually increased, the frog will fail to perceive the impending danger and ultimately meet its demise by being cooked alive.

> The real question is not, "Why pursue excellence?" but "What makes you feel compelled to strive for a greater standard of personal excellence?"

This metaphor perfectly encapsulates the consequences of embracing mediocrity. It depicts a person slowly dying inside themselves – only they're still here physically.

Fortunately, you still possess the option to escape the lukewarm waters and strive for your dreams, your enthusiasm, and your life's purpose. This endeavor demands unwavering commitment, unwavering dedication, unwavering focus, and unwavering devotion. Ultimately, the decision lies in your hands. It is a decision to do more and be more.

Reliable people can be counted upon to do what is expected of them, but excellent people habitually do more than asked. Persons of excellence deliver results in a way that leaves others around them pleasantly surprised.

"Do you see a man who excels in his work? He will stand before kings; he will not stand before unknown men." (Prov. 22:29) King Solomon has pointed out that laziness and apathy will get you nowhere, but hard work will open doors.

Once an individual has developed a mindset and set a standard of excellence, they will be the ones summoned by presidents and top officials to undertake exceptional endeavors, much like Rowan. The world is waiting for more people Rowans.

Now ask yourself:

Are you Rowan?
Are you living like Rowan?
Are you driven and focused?
Do you have a victorious attitude?
Do you strive for excellence in every task?
If not, what do you need to change?
How do you strive for excellence?
Do you cultivate excellence in all areas of your life?
Can you carry a message to Garcia?

Colin Powell once stated, "If you are going to achieve excellence in big things, you develop the habit in little matters. Excellence is not an exception; it is a prevailing attitude."

Merely meeting expectations should not be our ultimate objective. Striving for mediocrity, just to conform to societal norms, is not wise. It is like a professional baseball player aspiring to be on a t-ball team.

Regrettably, many individuals believe they are incapable of accomplishing great things, so they settle for mediocrity. They resign themselves to average standards. However, aiming for mediocrity will likely result in subpar outcomes. Instead, it is crucial to consistently raise the bar and foster a culture of high standards.

Throughout my entire professional career, I have consistently harbored a deep passion for leading a life of excellence. I continuously strive to expand my value, uphold ethical principles, exert diligent efforts, and maximize productivity, all while maintaining high standards to foster these qualities. I believe that if you're going to put your name on it, make sure that when it goes out, you won't want to take it back. I don't let others hold me back. Whenever someone claims that a task cannot be accomplished or it is impossible, I will be the first one in line to figure out why they are wrong.

I embrace life with an unwavering zeal and passion. Even during moments in life when I don't feel like it, and my enthusiasm plummets, I consciously focus to remain excited and enthusiastic.

> If you're going to put your name on it, make sure that when it goes out, you won't want to take it back.

I have consistently strived to exceed the expectations set by the world, always going the extra mile. Therefore, I present you with a challenge: go above and beyond by doing 10% more. One of the key methods to stand out and reach greatness is to elevate your personal standards. Look at what your job requires of you and then ascertain what an extra 10 percent would look like. Imagine the possibilities if you were to give just a little bit more of yourself. Set this as your new standard and pursue it with determination!

Let me ask you this question: Would you have your job if the place you work had a sign when you applied that read: "Wanted: Men and women like Lieutenant Rowan"?

A STANDARD OF EXCELLENCE

I have consistently found myself inspired by organizations and companies that seek to surpass common standards and achieve unparalleled excellence in their field. One of the first organizations that comes to my mind is NASA. They are a great model of exceptional exemplar of greatness.

In 1969, the Saturn V rocket, known for putting Neil Armstrong and Buzz Aldrin on the surface of the moon was launched. The 3-stage 363-foot rocket used its 7.5 million pounds of thrust to propel them into space and into history. The Saturn V was longer than a football field and was comprised of some 5,600,000 separate parts, all of which had to work perfectly to enable the rocket to carry out its mission.

However, in 1967, before it took Armstrong and Aldrin to the moon, the Saturn V flew as an unmanned flight. On the Apollo IV mission, the Saturn V flew a model flight with only two anomalies occurring. In short, it demonstrated a reliability of 99.9999%. Had the reliability of the flight only been 99%, there would have been 5,600 defective parts.

Regardless of how you analyze it, that is a remarkable demonstration of excellence and should serve as a source of encouragement to others. The presence of a foundation of excellence is imperative for any organization to advance successfully. NASA anticipates and requires top-notch performance from its employees in order to showcase excellence. Excellence is found in the details and in doing the small things well.

They do not demand perfection, as it is not attainable. However, they do expect employees to take responsibility for their actions. It is a commitment and dedication to achieving excellence.

Are You Committed to Excellence?

Personal excellence does not revolve around achieving perfection, but rather focuses on continuous growth. It is not a goal to be reached, a project to prove anything to anyone or unnecessarily stressing ourselves out. Personal excellence is a conscious decision to exceed expectations and surpass the status quo.

It is crucial to comprehend that excellence and perfection are not synonymous. Despite their frequent association or assumption of being intertwined, they possess distinct characteristics. Personal excellence does not revolve around achieving perfection, but rather focuses on continuous growth. It should not be perceived as a target to be attained or a means to impress others, as this would only lead to unnecessary stress. Excellence is using your unique God given talents to excel and shine. It is finding your passion to strive for your purpose and to do so with zeal.

We need to understand that it is okay not to be perfect and realize we will make mistakes. That is okay. Had Lt. Rowan got injured or even worse, it wouldn't have made him a failure. There are many people of excellence that were not able to achieve their mission at no fault of their own. What makes them people of excellence is their attitude and mindset. It is the determination to go forward and be their best self. Personal excellence is a conscious decision to rise above and go forward.

Do not strive for perfection, but rather strive for progress. Aim to make today better than yesterday so that tomorrow can be even better. The unwavering pursuit of improvement will propel anyone to greater heights.

Attaining greatness requires a lifelong commitment to personal growth. The pursuit of personal excellence involves striving for something greater within yourself in order to showcase your best self. It entails giving your utmost effort to reveal your true potential. It involves recognizing your strengths and weaknesses, identifying areas that require improvement, and cultivating positive habits.

Excellence is the continual pursuit of self-improvement in all aspects of life, including relationships and mindset. Are you actively seeking it?

Let me ask you a question: *If you're not dedicated to excellence, then what exactly are you dedicated to?*

The answer is simple. If you are not dedicated to excellence, you are bound to mediocrity. An attitude of 'mediocrity' is the enemy of excellence! You must break every chain of mediocrity that confines you from greatness and drowns you in a sea of average.

Excellence is not about *HAVING* to be the best; it's doing *YOUR* best! It is an opportunity to tap into your talents, living with passion and fulfilling your God-given purpose. Excellence is not an act, but a habit.

Unfortunately, mediocrity exists and floods our streets. It has become an acceptable standard. It not only lives but thrives all around us. We see it in our workplace, our homes, our schools, our churches, and the places we shop. 'Okay' is not okay. Good enough isn't good enough.

Often, we tend to overlook the significant impact that other people's decision to simply get by can have on us. Think about flying in an airplane. As you soar through the skies, thousands of feet above the ground, how would you feel if you knew that the individuals responsible for constructing the aircraft put in the same level of effort, integrity, and energy as you do in your own responsibilities and job? Would you be comforted or a little worried?

Now, imagine if the person responsible for tightening the nuts and bolts on the wing of the plane you are flying in only gave 95% of their effort. What if you were aware that this individual didn't truly care about delivering their personal best? What if they disregarded the importance of maintaining a standard of excellence with each screw and bolt they worked on? Picture this worker zipping through assembling the wing of your plane as quickly as they could, daydreaming about something else int their life. As they zoom through each bolt, they say something like, "Well, it's good enough. I think that bolt will hold." Would you be worried? I know I would! I am confident that every individual reading this would share similar apprehensions.

Consider this alternative scenario. Imagine you decide you are going skydiving. Which person would you want to pack your parachute? ? In one room a person was packing the chutes, doing so carefully and accurately, giving attention to every detail. In the other room, was a person listening to loud music, distracted by constant interruptions on their phone, and rushing to get the chute packed so they can go get some pizza to eat. Which person would you get the chute from?

Why do people willingly choose the dark cloak of mediocrity when they can shine like the stars? What propels people to continue laboring under its weight, without wanting to break free? Unfortunately, too often people settle low and are satisfied with average. They stop trying hard and just want to get by. That includes the guy who built your plane or packed your chute.

So, I will return to my question. Are you committed to a level of excellence? Or are you like the person who did an average job putting your plane together or packing a chute?

Anyone can exceed expectations once in a while, the key is to do it consistently. Resist the urge to do only what is expected of you. It is important to resist the temptation of merely meeting the expected standards. Instead, dedicate your utmost effort to every task at hand, and you will witness remarkable outcomes.

Instead of merely meeting expectations, one can aspire to surpass them. This is where the thrill lies, and where one can truly make a difference. It is the starting point of greatness, radiating its brilliance upon you. The key to unlocking personal excellence lies in the commitment to rise above and strive for one's utmost potential. Believe it or not, the kind of questions you ask yourself affects the life you lead.

So now look at yourself.

1. Are you striving for personal excellence?
2. Are you surpassing a level of excellence in all you do?
3. Are you committed and disciplined to keep going?
4. Are you utilizing all your skills and qualities at a level which is above the standards?
5. What do you need to do to reach your goals?

Let me ask you these questions:
What do you stand for?
What do you want to be known for?
What standards have you set for yourself?
What is your purpose?

Purpose fuels your motivation. What do you look forward to achieving tomorrow, month or in the next five years? Imagine waking up every day passionate and excited for what you've set out to accomplish. That emotion alone will propel you to the next level.

Every morning, you are faced with two options: To drag yourself out of bed and go through the motions of your day; or, to rise up and chase after all the opportunities ahead of you with zeal.

There exist individuals in the world who aspire to accomplish remarkable feats in their lives, yet they lack the determination to exert the necessary effort to get there. They want success but are not willing to do what it takes to get there. While the rest of the world is sitting on their sofas watching reruns of their favorite television show, people of excellence are working on their goals, achieving their dreams.

There are three types of people:
1) People who jump in and make things happen.
2) People who hope things might happen.
3) People who dream of what could happen.

Which person do you want to be? My guess is that since you are reading this book, you want to be a person who makes things happen and excel.

This means going outside of your comfort zone. It means going places where you know you will be at a disadvantage and a challenge. Step beyond the boundaries. Compete against superior performers. Engage in competition with individuals who excel in their performance. Observe, read, listen, and analyze the distinctive approaches adopted by individuals like the Rowans. The secret to success lies in the very thing you're avoiding. If you want long-term success, stop avoiding what's hard, and embrace it now.

Few people achieve greatness not because they lack talent, drive or ability, but because they lack perseverance, resilience, and the willingness to go through and grow from pain.

There's a saying for athletes, that the workout doesn't start until pain arrives. This principle also holds true for individuals striving to meet Garcia standards.

To truly excel, one must be prepared to confront and overcome challenges and difficulties and embrace them. It requires perseverance and the willingness to keep going, even when the desire to quit is strong. True greatness is a commitment that is upheld every day, even during the most difficult times. Achieving excellence and greatness is not a destination, but rather a journey that is undertaken with determination and resilience.

A forgotten man named Rowan, serves as a reminder that the world yearns for individuals who can set aside their personal achievements and acknowledge that the ultimate objective is never truly attained. They don't let the illusion of success overtake them. They keep going and persistently strive for greatness.

> Get to excellence, then sustain excellence.

The key to accomplishment in Hubbard's story is caught when he writes, "It is not book-learning young men need, nor instruction about this or that, but a stiffening of the vertebrae which will cause them to be loyal to a trust, to act promptly, concentrate their energies; do the thing."[ii]

It is appalling, the number of people who are content with 'average' and mediocre. There are too many people who will only do the minimum expected of them! They see no reason why they should have to do more than is required of them. Some people work harder to do less, when instead they would put the same energy into giving more, they would achieve greater victory. These people will never get a message to their Garcia. Let's face it, they'll never even know who Garcia is, let alone be summoned to pass on any message.

In order to get what you've never had, you must do what you've never done. To get what you've never had, you must do what you've never done. This simply means rising up and going beyond your limits. It requires the ability to perceive beyond the current circumstances and having the determination to discover a means to achieve it. It entails stepping outside of your comfort zone to accomplish the task at hand. The objective is to reach a state of excellence and maintain it consistently. This is precisely why Rowan was chosen for his significant undertaking.

A lack of drive is not uncommon in people. Numerous individuals are satisfied with a mindset of just getting by, doing the bare minimum. They are content with being content. Complacency is the enemy of success. It is a silent killer. To rise above mediocrity, we must step outside the norm and comfort zone, and embrace a better way to think, act and live.

It is essential to acknowledge that living each day with a purpose is crucial. Individuals who possess the ability to effectively convey a message to Garcia are truly exceptional. I assure you that if you give yourself permission to pursue what's important to you with zeal, you will be sought after

The path to Garcia is not an easy and bright like the yellow brick road of the Wizard of Oz. The pursuit of excellence begins by pushing and challenging yourself to strive for personal growth and improvement. It is a journey that requires varying degrees of effort and determination, but it always serves as a test of one's own abilities and the ability to surpass internal boundaries.

Remember this: An attitude of 'mediocre' is the enemy of excellence!

In the midst of our hectic and busy daily schedules, the grind of our routines and battle to get things done, it is easy to lose sight of excellence. Our minds become consumed by never-ending to-do lists, errands, and the constant pressure to meet expectations. We all could come up with a list of excuses as to why we are so busy! But the reality is, we either are committed to a daily act of excellence, or we are not.

One day I began wondering about the time when I reach the later stages of my life, will I reflect and feel remorseful for not giving certain aspects of my life my utmost effort. I have reached an age where I can evaluate the path I have taken and the obstacles I have encountered. However, I am still at a stage where I can bring about a transformation. And for you, if you are alive and breathing, you possess the capability to initiate that transformation. The reality is that personal growth is an ongoing journey without a definitive endpoint.

When looking back on your life, do you discern any areas where you feel you could have allocated more attention? Are there any aspects you wish you had done better? Different? With more zeal? With more passion?

I'd like to ask you a question: Where in your life have you been doing less than your best? Where have you set the bar? Are you willing to commit to becoming a better version of yourself – a person of excellence. Are you prepared to eliminate anything in your life that falls short of excellence?

Choose today to transition from being satisfactory to becoming exceptional. Devote yourself to moving from good to great. Commit yourself to surpassing the status quo and striving for excellence.

Excellence is a daily commitment, not a one-off task.

Today, I want to challenge you to:

Develop a passion for excellence.

Engage your passion and purpose.

Explore new ways of personal growth with passion.

Ignite your passion for excellence to reach your purpose.

The extent of your accomplishments is directly influenced by your actions and the level of proficiency you exhibit. Attainable objectives can be reached when you exert maximum effort and dedicate yourself entirely.

The extent of your accomplishments is directly influenced by your actions and the level of proficiency you exhibit. It depends on what you do and how well you do it. Attainable objectives can be reached when you exert maximum effort and dedicate yourself entirely. A high degree of enthusiasm, zeal, and determination significantly enhances your accomplishments.

Excellence, Prosperity, Abundance. Your name is synonymous with these qualities. I present to you a challenge today - embrace a lifestyle of excellence. Transform into an individual who distinguishes themselves and is entrusted with the responsibility of delivering a message to Garcia. The world eagerly anticipates and observes individuals like Rowan. Will you rise to the occasion and become one of them?

Excellence is a part of who you are.
It defines you.
It is something that makes
you stand out
in the crowd.

– Jason R. Doll

An Attitude of Excellence

THE PURSUIT OF EXCELLENCE

I find it difficult to comprehend how individuals can get out of bed and start their day without aspiring to attain personal excellence and strive for success in all they do. I fail to understand how someone can consciously choose to merely survive the day instead of thriving. I question why anyone would desire such an outlook.

When I wake up in the mornings, I purposefully choose to ignite my inner self and proceed forward with an optimistic mindset. Even when I am facing my toughest days, I make a choice to focus on having a positive attitude.

Your attitude can be a game-changer, determining whether you will succeed or be held back from pursuing your passions and fulfilling your purpose. It is the lens through which you view and react to life's circumstances, interactions with others, and even your own self. Remember, your attitude is not something that happens to you, it is choose by you. You have the power to shape your mindset and determine how you will interpret and handle the ups and downs of life. Ultimately, it is up to you to decide whether your outlook will be positive or negative.

If I were to ask you, what does having an attitude of excellence mean to you, how would you answer? Personally, I believe that maintaining an "attitude of excellence" establishes the benchmark for how I live my life. It entails purposefully perceiving, contemplating, and reacting. It is intentional. Excellence is ingrained in my identity and serves as a defining characteristic.

Simply put: Excellence is something that makes you stand out in a crowd. It is an attitude.

No matter how you define personal excellence, it starts in your mind – and it is revealed through your attitude.

Excellence is a part of you, something that defines you. It is something that makes you stand out in a crowd. It is an attitude, a choice. In fact, one's attitude is probably the most impacting of all human qualities. It must be infused into everything we do.

> Excellence is a part of you, something that defines you. It is something that makes you stand out in a crowd. It is an attitude, a choice.

The power of your mind is immense. Undoubtedly, your mind serves as the utmost crucial asset in leading a life of excellence. It all begins within our minds. Excellence is not merely a skill, but rather an outlook and an attitude.

Individuals who achieve success are able to generate superior results due to their optimistic and proactive mindset. Their thoughts are not overwhelmed or distracted by negativity, cynicism, or pessimism. By consciously adopting a mindset of excellence, you will accomplish more, experience greater enjoyment, foster stronger relationships, prioritize your physical and mental well-being, and significantly enhance the overall quality of your daily existence. You have complete and total control over your attitude every waking moment.

He tells Luke Skywalker, "Do or do not...there is no try." This simple statement holds a profound truth – either you accomplish something, or you do not. Yoda emphasizes the importance of believing in oneself and eliminating any doubts about achieving one's goals. Essentially, he encourages us to strive for excellence by expecting nothing less than our best.

Individuals who achieve the greatest success make a conscious choice to take full control of their attitude. They firmly believe that no external factor or other people can deprive them of this power!

If you speak with any Olympic athlete, they will tell you that they never go out and compete with the thoughts of "trying" their best. Their objective is to do nothing less than their best. They push themselves to rise above. They dig down deep when they don't think they can give more, and they find the strength to keep going. Before they ever step out to compete, they have already made their mindset to rise up and be the best.

> An attitude of complacency is the enemy of excellence!

You have to be determined to maintain the right attitude and mindset – unwavering and determined. Greek philosopher Aristotle said, "We are what we repeatedly do. Excellence, therefore, is not an act, but a habit." By consistently demonstrating excellence, one can cultivate a pattern of exemplary behavior. It is important to recognize that complacency poses a significant threat to achieving greatness. Never forget that an attitude of complacency is the enemy of excellence!

The power of attitude cannot be underestimated. One of the most famous stories in the Bible that highlights the significance of a person's attitude and mindset is the account of Moses sending 12 spies to scout the land of Canaan before the Israelites went there to live. Their mission was to observe and gather information about the land and its inhabitants. They were to see what it was like. How many were there? They were tasked with assessing the strength of the people and determining if the land could be conquered. Moses encouraged them and told them to 'be of good courage' (be brave) and bring back some of the fruit from the land.

But the other 10 spies spoke differently, displaying a horrible attitude about the whole endeavor and gave a completely different report. These men saw things different than Joshua and Caleb and began protesting the "people are a lot stronger than us. We can't win against them! They are tall like giants, and we are like grasshoppers!" After their report, the people began grumbling. Then Caleb silenced the people and said, "We should go up and take possession of the land, for we can certainly do it." The problem was, the people were caught in the tide of a defeated mindset.

Following a 40-day exploration of Canaan, the explorers presented their findings. Joshua and Caleb returned with an enthusiastic and positive report. They informed the people that the land was abundant in resources and fertile, "flowing with milk and honey." They testified with great excitement and zeal, affirming their belief that they "We can conquer the land".

However, the other 10 spies gave a completely different perspective, displaying a negative attitude about their adventure. They provided a completely contrasting report from Joshua and Caleb, and began protesting, claiming that the people inhabiting the land were much stronger than them. They believed that victory was unattainable, "We should go up and take possession of the land, for we can certainly do it." Upon hearing this report, the people started grumbling.

In response, Caleb stepped forward and silenced the people. He confidently stated that they should proceed and seize the land, "We should go up and take possession of the land, for we can certainly do it."

The problem was, the people were caught in the tide of a defeated mindset, swept away by negative thoughts and doubts.

The outcome? The Israelites' pessimistic attitude an outlook had a detrimental impact on God's promises, to crumble right before them. Due to their toxic influence of the 10 spies, the Israelites were forced to return to the wilderness to wonder until they died. God postponed the fulfillment of His plan for His chosen people for a frustrating period of 40 years. However, Caleb and Joshua survived to witness a new era and, alongside a new generation, they were able to witness the fulfillment of God's promise in the Promised Land. (Numbers 14)

What caused the 10 spies' report to be entirely different? How is it possible that all the spies witnessed the exact same thing but came back with completely different reports? The only difference between the reports was their mindset. The negative attitudes of these ten individuals contaminated the entire congregation, causing anxiety to spread throughout the camp uncontrollably. Instead of placing trust in Joshua and Caleb's positive report, which would have led to victory, they clung to uncertainty and remained mentally oblivious and blind.

This story provides an important lesson: Your mindset and attitude has the potential to hinder, obstruct, or delay your progress towards attaining your goal or purpose It is imperative to embrace a mental attitude that forces you to keep moving forward.

Today, in the world, we still have these two groups of people. Some can see the opportunities and have the disposition that says, "We are able! We are capable! We can!" While there are other groups of people who can only see the flaws and doubts stating, "I am skeptical. We are not able. We can't."

Let us look deeper into the two groups and examine their characteristics. The first group consists of ten spies who possess a negative attitude, which defines their character.

The ten spies' attitude were:

(1) Doubt. They said, "We are not able to!"
(2) Self-depreciation. They saw themselves as insignificant and tiny compared to the other people.
(3) Fear. Fear paralyzed them and kept them from acting.
(4) Critical spirit. When people become discouraged or idle, they turn to criticizing those going forward.
(5) Rebellion. They rebelled against their purpose of going to where they were called to go.
(6) Ingratitude. They failed to appreciate all that they had and could have.
(7) Unbelief. All of these negative traits can be summed up in one word - unbelief.

Now, let us examine the demeanor of Caleb and Joshua. They possessed a positive perspective and approach:

(1) Positive Outlook - Caleb and Joshua were able to see possibilities and opportunities instead of focusing on the negative and barriers.
(2) Confidence. They said, "We are well able to overcome it." They believed in themselves, in fellow Israelites and God. They believed they could overcome the difficulties.
(3) Conquering Attitude -They were courageous warriors, willing and ready to fight for their goal and purpose.
(4) Faith. They believed in their calling and the outcome of this undertaking. They trusted their God.
(5) Courage. They were not afraid of the giants, walled city, or the strength of the people already there.
(6) Action. Caleb said, "Let us go at once, and possess it." Positive people -like Rowan- say, "Let's go and do it!"
(7) Thankfulness. They truly appreciate what they had and what could be theirs.

If you aspire to achieve excellence, it is crucial not to emulate the behavior of the ten spies. A negative attitude will impede your ability to reach your full potential. It will restrain your progress towards your goals and purpose, diminish your enthusiasm, create distance between you and your loved ones, and have a detrimental impact on all aspects of your life. However, it is important to remember that you have the power to change this situation.

Remember this important truth: You are unique and distinct from everyone else. You possess exceptional qualities that set you apart. You are a cut above. Your purpose is to strive for greatness, surpassing ordinary expectations. It is God's desire for you to establish the utmost level of excellence in every aspect of your life.

> When your attitude shifts, everything in your world shifts.

You must strive to become an exemplary employee within your organization. It is crucial for both your supervisor and colleagues to recognize your outstanding qualities and exceptional work ethic. Wouldn't you desire to be the kind of employee that your boss admires and encourages others to emulate? Wouldn't you like your boss to tell others about you, "Watch them closely. Follow their example. This person is the cream of the crop!"?

If you lack the same skills, training, opportunities, or education as your peers, it is of no consequence as long as you possess an attitude of excellence. You can still rise up and be the one called upon, like Rowan.

During the early stages of my professional journey, I had a tendency to frequently approach my manager and ask about every little thing I could. I consistently sought guidance and direction, constantly asking questions like "What is the correct approach for this task?" or "Is there a better way of doing this?" I was eager to discover more efficient ways of accomplishing tasks. Unfortunately, my company did not offer a training program, leaving me untrained and unsure of where to begin. Due to my lack of experience, I was unaware of the mindset and decision-making process of a leader, and what they might have done differently in similar situations.

Luckily, I discovered the solution buried within. I learned to be a solver of problems rather than a conveyor of problems. I wanted to create solutions, not just bring questions. That is when I made a choice. A choice to be different, think differently and live intentionally. I made a decision. I chose to be unique, to adopt a different mindset, and to live purposefully.

When I learned to change my mindset, instead of raising concerns, and problems, I approached my manager with innovative ideas and practical solutions. I would inform them about the challenges we faced and then explain how I successfully resolved or planned to solve them. As a result, their workload became more manageable, and I started to distinguish myself from others.

I transitioned from being someone who was a 'problem asker' to a 'problem solver'. I started taking care of issues that weren't mine, even when no one asked. I began turning challenges into opportunities.

It's no coincidence that shortly afterwards, I began standing out. Suddenly, I found myself on a trend of being recommended for promotions all the way to leading large organizations. But it started with the pursuit of excellence.

Throughout my professional journey, particularly in my positions of leadership, I have consistently emphasized the importance to my employees about utilizing to bring their knowledge, creativity, and experience to their areas of work in order to solve problems and identify opportunities. I didn't discourage them from asking questions, I encouraged them - but, when appropriate. I want them to grow by first looking for the solution, then asking questions.

By adopting a problem-solving mindset rather than being a source of problems, you will distinguish yourself as a valuable asset within the organization. As you strive for excellence and maintain high standards, you will witness new doors of opportunity opening up before you.

The attitude you think in is the life you will live in. Remember this: The way you think is the way you will do everything. It is critical for you to grasp this. Your mindset is one of the most important self-obtained predictors of your life.

> Our attitudes are an outward display of what's taking place inside our hearts.

Your perspective on life will determine how you respond to trials and triumphs. It is a choice. We are not slaves to our attitude; we have power over it.

A negative mindset can be considered the greatest hindrance in our life. Maintaining a positive outlook is effortless when everything is going smoothly in life. However, when you encounter unexpected setbacks and difficulties, the way you respond demonstrates to the world around you what is really in your heart. It is during these trying moments and challenging times when you discover if you have what it takes to get a message to Garcia.

There are endless possibilities for what you can achieve, and it all begins with a paradigm shift in your mindset and attitude. Changing your attitude might be easier than you think. Through commitment and self-control, you have the ability to "reprogram" your thoughts.

The great American psychologist, William James of Harvard University, once said, "Human beings can alter their lives by altering their attitudes of mind."

Abraham Lincoln said: "Folks are usually about as happy as they make their minds up to be."

Both these quotes are spot on and something we should embrace in our daily life.

How do you begin your day when you wake up in the morning? Do you get up and go out with an optimistic, energetic, and encouraged attitude? Or do you get up moping around, dreading the day ahead of you before it even begins? Are you focused on the victories or the worries of your day? How do you initiate your day?

Over the years, I have had the privilege of conversing with numerous individuals who have achieved great success in their respective fields. These include self-made multi-millionaires, prominent business figures, astronauts, Olympic medalists, accomplished coaches, and influential world leaders. Interestingly, they all attribute their success to a common factor: the cultivation of a positive, victorious, and successful mindset. They program their minds to focus and operate at a higher level of positive thinking. They understand that to succeed, they must first have an attitude of excellence woven into their mindset.

Research has indicated that individuals who possessed the belief that they could achieve a specific objective successfully accomplished their desired outcome in 93% of cases.

Don't pull yourself down in worry. Worrying wastes your energy and actually hurts you. It never gets you anywhere. It simply binds you, restricting you from moving towards your goals. Stop worrying about something you have no control over. Studies show that 80% of the things we worry about never actually materialize.

Regardless of the challenges you may be facing, it is crucial to acknowledge that you possess the ability to consciously opt for a positive and hopeful outlook. It can be a simple matter of perspective. Obstacles are often camouflaged and disguise hidden opportunities. Once you adopt this mindset, your entire viewpoint can undergo a significant shift. Consequently, your entire future has the potential to be completely transformed.

The Bible expresses in Proverbs 23:7 this same concept: "As a man thinks in his heart, so is he." What Solomon is telling us in this passage is that God has given us the ability to program ourselves for abundant living.

How are you supposed to keep an attitude of victory in this crazy, unpredictable world? Well, you must begin looking at the world differently.

Here is what an attitude of excellence requires:

1. Optimism. It doesn't mean ignoring your problems or denying the existence of adversity. Instead, it allows you to deal with challenging situations more productively.
2. Positive Attitude. Despite the hardships in life, a positive attitude will allow you to be much happier, and you will be able to see the good around you.
3. Reliable. In an era where a signed contract can even be broken, trust is a treasure. Being certain that someone will show up on time "come rain or shine" and do what they have promised to do is a priceless quality.
4. Resilience. Being able to bounce back from adversity, disappointment, and failure instead of giving up.
5. Acceptance. Sometimes, despite your best efforts, things just don't work out. In those circumstances, acceptance can help you grow and move forward.

6. Intentional. Have a mindset to be deliberate in all that you do. Intentional excellence starts in your mind.
7. Gratitude. Being thankful is an important aspect of a positive attitude.
8. Grow. Your mindset must allow you to grow. Daily. Do not be stagnant.

The caliber of your life is determined by the quality of your thoughts. Your mindset holds immense power and is crucial in attaining personal excellence. With the correct mindset, there are no limits to what you can accomplish. Embracing a triumphant and constructive mindset will propel you towards excellence, serving as a launching pad for success.

We must constantly strive to become the finest version of ourselves. It is imperative that we uphold the standard of excellence, beginning with our own character. If we do not dedicate ourselves to becoming our best selves, then what is our true commitment?

Allow me to pose this question: If everyone possessed the same attitude as you, how would the world appear? Would it be better or worse?

Imagine tomorrow you wake up and go to your kitchen to make breakfast. You sit down at the table and open up the paper or your electronic device and right there in front of you is your own obituary. There, in black and white, is your name.

Imagine being seated in your kitchen chair, and you look down and read your own obituary! would it say? How would it be read? What would it convey about the way you led your life? Would it have positive things to say? What would it say about all the things you did with your life? Would you feel a sense of pride in what was written, or would you want for the opportunity to have accomplished more in your lifetime?

That is exactly what happened on April 13, 1888 to Alfred Nobel. Nobel woke up to experience an unexpected turn of events. Upon waking up, he was confronted with an unsettling revelation on the front page of the morning newspaper. As he looked at the newspaper, he came face to face with an article reporting his own death. Because of a misunderstanding, the local newspaper mistakenly believed that Mr. Nobel had passed away. However, this incident provided Mr. Nobel with a unique insight into the perception of his life by others.

As Mr. Nobel read his obituary, he didn't like what he saw. The portrayal of his life horrified him. Nobel at that moment realized two things: One, that what was depicted in the paper was how he was going to be remembered forever. Second, this was not how he wanted to be remembered. In that very moment, he decided to redesign his name. He decided to change his legacy and restore his reputation.

After that day, Mr. Nobel decided to change a lot of things in his life. One contribution he established was creating the Nobel Peace Prize, aimed at acknowledging exceptional achievements of individuals. Today, Alfred Nobel is not remembered for his past negative conduct, but rather for all he did to help others in an extraordinary way.

Consider this scenario: You open the newspaper and come across your own obituary. Take a moment to reflect on this thought. If you were to pass away today, what would your obituary reveal? How would your loved ones and friends encapsulate the essence of your entire life?

What would your legacy be?

Would people remember your passion, zeal, inspiration, and love for others? Or would they remember your negative attitude, your short temper, your sharp tongue?

What would they remember about your life?

Would they remember you as an inspiration to others?

What type of mark would they say you left behind in this wonderful world?

Would you be known as a person of excellence?

Would they say you fulfilled your God-given purpose?

Would they call you a Rowan?

These are challenging and direct questions. However, they are questions that will sooner or later be asked. How will your obituary someday be written? What would you like it to convey? What and how will you be remembered for?

We have an easy tendency to look at the world through a short-term lens. We focus our energy on today's schedules, events, and expenses. It becomes easy to rush through our days and pay no attention to our lasting legacy. Each day, you are leaving a thumbprint in life and on other people's lives.

Research shows that people over 50 years old, when asked, "If you could live your life over again, what would you do differently?" generally responded, "If I had it to do over again, I would reflect more, pursue more, risk more, enjoy more, and leave legacy for after I am dead."

A few decades from now, when you look back through all the years behind you, as the flashbacks come slowly filling your mind, what will you see? What legacy will you leave behind?

I've often wondered how my obituary will be read. What will it say? What type of life have I lived that impacted the world around me?

The good news is you can still write your story. There is still time. If you are alive, you have a purpose! How you live and what you do with what is left allows you to write the story of your life. Right now, you have an opportunity to live intentionally! How will you write your obituary? It depends on how you will live your life.

Years ago, I had a professor who told me a well-known story of a man who was out walking and found an abandoned eagle's egg. Concerned for its safety, he picked it up and took it home where he placed it in his chicken coop. Over time, the egg hatched alongside the baby chickens.

The young eaglet began its life with his new family – the chickens. He associated itself and grew up with all the other chickens in the coop, learning and doing whatever they did.

As the eagle matured, he continued to mimic and live like the chickens. Since the chickens could only fly for a short distance, the eagle only flew a short distance. Since the chickens stayed in the coop, the eagle never left either. He believed that he was what he saw. He was living the same way as his environment. He believed that all he could do was what the chickens could do. Consequently, he didn't know how much more he was actually able to do.

One day the eagle looked up to see a bird flying high above him. He was amazed how high it was. "How is he doing that?" the eagle asked one of the older chickens.

"That's an eagle." the hen told him. "He is the mightiest and greatest of all us birds. He belongs to the sky." The eagle in the sky looked down to see the young eagle in the coop and wondered why he was there. So, he flew down to rest upon the chicken coop and asked the young eagle, "What are you doing in this chicken coop?" The youthful eagle replied, "This is my home. I've grown up here." The mature eagle replied, "You are an eagle, not a chicken! You are mighty and strong. You can fly like me, and your home is high up among the cliffs, not here in a coop! You are meant for more than just living in a coop. You were made to soar."

Immediately, the young eagle decided that he did not want to be stuck on the ground in the dirt like the chickens. He decided to shed his mindset as a chicken, and instead be an eagle. As a result, he took to the sky, soared to great heights, and lived his best life.

So, why was the younger eagle grounded for such a long time? Why did he decide to remain confined, residing alongside the other chickens? It was because he made the conscious decision to associate himself with the chickens rather than embracing his true potential.

Each and every one of us is born with the innate ability to soar high and unrestricted above the clouds, just like an eagle. Nevertheless, numerous individuals choose to live among the chickens, never venturing beyond the ground. They are content just being with the other chickens in their life.

There is a stark difference between living as a chicken or as an eagle. Chickens are not the cutest birds and can be very messy and stinky. Whereas eagles are gorgeous, majestic, and elegant.

Chickens are confined to coops, leading a stagnant existence. On the other hand, eagles roam freely among treetops and mountain peaks, traversing vast distances.

Chickens constantly gaze downward, pecking at the dirty, duty ground, eating any bugs they can find. Conversely, eagles perpetually cast their gaze skyward, perching majestically in lofty locations high above, remaining vigilant and surveying their surroundings for prey, for they are the predator.

Chickens walk and can barely fly five feet off the ground. Where eagles seldom walk and instead prefer to soar gracefully at altitudes reaching up to 10,000 feet At such heights, they surpass other birds who struggle to breathe. With regal grace, eagles glide above the clouds and mountain peaks, effortlessly navigating through the air like royalty.

Chickens are small, scrawny, and easy prey. While the eagle spreads his wings, he is nearly ten feet long and as he soars high above the mountains, he is the hunter and not the prey.

A chicken can only see up to a few feet in distance with limited vision. Whereas eagles can see their prey from up to 3 miles away. Their vision is incredible to see both great distances and what's right around them. We know that the view is limited to the ground in a coop, but from the air you can see greater distances.

In a storm, a chicken will hide and find shelter to remove itself from the tempest. An eagle on the other hand, will fly high above the storm, rising over the clouds, and uses the storm to its advantage.

Chickens are attacked by snakes which come to eat their eggs. Conversely, an eagle will capture a snake and fly high with it in its claws to kill it and eat it.

Like our young eagle friend in the story above, many people are living with chickens, and they do not even realize it. They are living like chickens. They lead a chicken-like existence, adopting the mindset, lifestyle, and even relationships of chickens. They raise their families as chickens, consume food like chickens, and ultimately meet their demise within the confines of a chicken coop. What many do not know is that they were designed to be an eagle and intended to soar to great things in their lives, but instead, they live restricted like chickens their entire life.

This is what I want you to grasp and dwell in: You were designed to be an eagle. You were destined to live a majestic life, and to soar high above the world achieving all you were created for.

'Soaring' is defined as: *to rise high in the air* and *increase rapidly above the usual level.*

Had this story gone the other direction, the young eagle would have missed out on what he was meant to be. He would have never found his purpose. In the same way, we must make sure that we become the person we were preordained to be. We must live our passion and purpose; we need to have a mindset and perform like eagles.

Every individual has gifts and talents that can make a lasting impact. However, only a minority of people utilize those gifts and talents to live up to their full potential.

I need to ask you to be honest with yourself and ask yourself the following, "Am I living in a chicken coop or am I living like the mighty eagle?"

Perhaps you were raised in a chicken coop. It's possible that your upbringing confined your perception of your capabilities, but now is the moment for the past to release its grip on you. It's time to escape from the coop and leave the chickens in the past. It's time to soar and accomplish your true calling.

You have choices about who you want to be and what you do next, just like the young eagle did. You get to decide if you will be in the chicken coop or fly high in the sky.

So, begs the question: Are you ready to get out of the coop and to live with passion? Are you ready to fulfill your purpose?

You were designed for a purpose greater than you can imagine. Your potential for success is directly linked to your ability to overcome obstacles and reach new heights. You were created for a life of excellence – not a life of mediocrity. Mediocrity is not in your nature; you were meant for greatness. Our Creator crafted you with a unique blend of passion and purpose. Today, you hold the power to shape your own destiny. Just like Mr. Nobel, you have the opportunity to write the next chapter of your life.

Now is where the rubber meets the road. It's up to you. Your time is now. No matter how bad things appear or how off course you seem to be in life, rest on this, it is never too late to make a change. What Happens next is up to you!

Currently, there might be individuals telling you to stop searching and simply be content. Some people will tell you to just be happy where you are. Others will attempt to stop you from trying to grow and get out of the chicken coop. They will try to persuade you just keep doing the same old thing over and over and over again. However, your purpose is greater. You were born to rise up and be free so you can fly to greater heights.

You are faced with a decision. The decision lies solely in your hands. You have the option to heed the advice of the chickens and remain firmly rooted. Alternatively, you can keep doing what you have been doing, or you can rise up and soar.

I believe that each one of us is born with a God-given purpose. Purpose shows you the path to take; it is the reason you journey forward to be all you desire. Your passion is the fire that lights the way to your purpose. This purpose serves as a guide, directing us towards the path we should tread, and it is the driving force behind our pursuit of fulfillment. Our passion acts as a beacon, illuminating the way towards our purpose. It provides us with the necessary motivation to persevere, even in the face of seemingly insurmountable obstacles. Passion is about "what," and purpose is about "why." We may harbor passion for various endeavors, but our purpose is typically singular and concentrated.

When passion is not connected with purpose, it leads to burnout.

When we embrace our passion, we naturally direct our attention towards our desires, igniting a sense of enthusiasm that effortlessly propels us forward. While passion serves as the initial driving force, it is a purpose that sustains our motivation and propels us to keep moving.

Many people claim that they face difficulties in discovering their purpose, but I believe it is right in front of you; you are simply disregarding it. What I am suggesting is that you are probably aware of your passion, you just might not be giving yourself permission to pursue it. Your purpose should bring forth joy within you and ignite a fervent passion. It is crucial to acknowledge your God-given purpose and seize it with both hands.

Having a purpose enables us to establish a personal mission, setting goals and determining the direction of our lives. Finding your purpose answers, the 'why'. Once we uncover and comprehend our purpose, our lives undergo a transformation. We begin to attract the things we have always desired in our life. Living your purpose is vital in every aspect of your life. Your purpose is so linked with your identity that the two can't be separated.

Purpose is what makes your passion sustainable. Finding purpose is to find meaning, and is not always a simple task. However, this difficulty does not diminish its importance. Anything worthwhile requires effort and is bound to be challenging.

Many people assert that they face difficulties in discovering their purpose, but I believe it is right in front of them; they simply choose to overlook it. What I am suggesting to you is that you are probably aware of your passion, you just might not be giving yourself permission to pursue it.

Perhaps you've provided a list of reasons for why you cannot. You may be too content with your current situation or too occupied with other commitments. Maybe you're hesitant to make the necessary changes in your life that would lead you to where you want to be and what you want to achieve. While some of your reasons may be valid, they ultimately serve as mere excuses.

It's important that you actively search for and embrace your own purpose. You can't simply adopt someone else's purpose and hope to find happiness by following their path. Instead, you need to define your own unique purpose in life.

Listening to others' opinions and seeking outside approval will never help you find your purpose. It's time to stop relying on others and their advice and start listening to what your heart is telling you – what is your purpose. If you constantly seek approval from others, you'll never be able to spread your wings and soar out of your comfort zone. Remember, everything you need to achieve your purpose is already within you. The only thing that's holding you back are your own limiting beliefs.

Let me pose a straightforward question: What drives your Passion, Purpose, and Reason in life?

Living your life with purpose and passion is irreplaceable. It's important to constantly ask yourself, "What motivates me? What brings joy to my heart?"

You possess a crucial role that only you can fulfill. You were designed to live a life of excellence - not a life of mediocrity or average. You are destined for more. Your moment is now. Instead of sitting around dreaming about your future, take action and chase after it. You are meant to soar and accomplish your dreams, goals, and purpose. It's your time to embrace life with enthusiasm, passion, and happiness.

Stop thinking and start acting. Choose to live a life of excellence. Embrace a life of greatness. When your goals align with your passions, you become unstoppable.

So, here's my last question:
What will you be remembered for?
What legacy will you leave behind?

What Comes Out, Is Inside

When you squeeze an orange, what comes out? Well, it's no surprise that you'll get orange juice. And when you squeeze a lemon, you'll get that tangy lemon juice. It's pretty obvious to everyone. What comes out is what's inside. Whatever is inside is what comes out. This metaphor is meant to help you reflect on what you're truly made of.

Putting someone under pressure is the most basic method of uncovering their true nature. When faced with a difficult situation that involves risk and stress, and having to make a decision, our response exposes what lies within us. The true measure of our inner thoughts and emotions becomes apparent during both the worst and best moments in our lives. Pressure doesn't build character, it reveals it. When we are squeezed, our words and actions reveal the truth.

I have personally witnessed both men and women react differently when confronted with the most challenging moments in life. Some choose to flee in fear, while others choose to confront the situation head-on. It is during these difficult times that our true selves and inner strength are revealed. We cannot conceal who we truly are when we find ourselves in the midst of a storm.

Lt. Rowan possesses a frequently underestimated quality in this tale. Despite facing immense pressure, he remained calm, cool, and collect. Despite encountering a challenging and seemingly impossible situation, Rowan's true character emerged and shone brightly. He persevered and pushed forward. As a result, he successfully accomplishes his mission.

Having a positive mindset is crucial because whatever is within you will eventually reveal itself. This is why cultivating a constructive attitude is so important. By maintaining a positive mental attitude, you can effectively handle challenging, stressful, and unfavorable circumstances in a healthier manner. It's not beneficial to fill yourself with toxic thoughts or emotions. That is why you need to make sure you are not surrounding yourself with negative people, toxic people, or those who are challenging you. When you're faced with pressure, these negative aspects will inevitably surface, often manifesting through your words and actions.

Our words reflect the direction of our hearts and thoughts. If bitterness fills you, it will be evident in your speech. Conversely, if your heart is filled with kindness, it will shine through your words.

We've all been guilty of it at some point – whining, complaining, criticizing, bellyaching, grumbling. It's become such a common part of our culture that we often don't even realize we're doing it. We find ourselves complaining about our jobs, the weather, school, our bosses, the slow Wi-Fi, the long lines, the heat, the cold, how fast things are, how slow things are, about the government, and our jam-packed schedules. We come home and complain about being single, or about the person we chose to marry. We complain about not having a job, but when we do have one, we find something to whine about - our coworkers. We complain about wanting a bigger house, but then when we have one we complain about having to clean it.

It's unfortunate that complaining has become so prevalent and accepted in our society. It's disheartening to see how complaining has become the norm and is widely tolerated.

Complaining has become deeply ingrained in our world, in our homes and in our lives, hindering our ability to fulfill our purpose and reach our full potential. It acts as a barrier to excellence, serving as one of the most detrimental forces we encounter. Surprisingly, it resides within our own minds.

We need to free ourselves from this kind of mindset, speaking, and lifestyle. Merely exerting more effort to be virtuous won't suffice as the underlying issue lies within us. This wise saying reveals the correlation between our words and thoughts. Luke 6:45 says, "The words that come out of our mouths are a reflection of what fills our hearts."

Research has revealed that criticism has the potential to negatively impact your physical, mental, emotional, and spiritual well-being. It fosters a toxic environment in our lives and dissuades our passions. Moreover, it undermines our sense of purpose and devours us from within.

I absolutely despise drama. I refuse to tolerate it, whether it's in my professional environment or my personal life. Why? Because it breads negativity, toxic components and destroys the fabrics of excellence. Complaining accomplishes nothing but wasting precious time for both you and me.

Complaining is counterproductive, my friend. Instead of wasting your precious energy and mental capacity on it, why not channel that power towards achieving your goals? By letting go of complaints, you free yourself to accomplish something truly meaningful. Remember, when you criticize, you divert your focus from what truly matters in your life.

When we read about Rowan, being summoned to search for Garcia deep in the jungle, he had every reason to complain. He could have grumbled about it not being his responsibility. He could have criticized his commanders for sending him into the wilderness without any guidance or direction. He could have questioned why they didn't choose someone else first. He could have complained about the bugs, the humid weather, the dangerous animals, and not knowing which way to go. He could have felt justified in venting to his friends and family about how impossible this mission seemed.

However, there's one important aspect to consider: Rowan never complained. He didn't whine to his crew as they navigated through the thick jungle. Instead, Rowan promptly embarked on the task assigned to him. And he accomplished it! He never paused to criticize the mission. He didn't dwell on the countless potential challenges that lay ahead. He didn't possess that kind of mindset. He fully grasped that if he got caught up in such matters, he would probably fail in his mission.

While complaining at certain times can be useful by releasing stress, more often it is often used as a means to avoid taking action and finding solutions. Instead of actively working towards resolving problems, people tend to complain in order to feel a sense of achievement, even though it is false. Rather than directly addressing rude individuals, we tend to complain about them to others.

Complaining often arises when we fixate on external factors that are beyond our control. We tend to express dissatisfaction when there is a noticeable disparity between our expectations and the actual situation. Instances such as other people's actions, future events, work methods, weather conditions, and various aspects of life are common triggers for complaints. Instead of seeking resolutions, individuals tend to direct their frustration towards unchangeable negative energy.

Remember, it's important to keep in mind that complaining and taking action are two completely different things. Simply whining about a problem won't solve it. Complaining is the opposite of being grateful. Instead of always finding faults, we have the choice to focus on things we can be thankful for.

Complaining behavior can have negative consequences and reflect a lack of strength in one's character. The issue with constantly griping is that it drains your energy. However, you have the power to break free from this cycle and thrive. Focus on the things that you can actually control when you find yourself in that state. By directing your energy towards these areas, you'll find less to complain about.

We all know someone who seems to always seems to find something to complain about. It can be quite exhausting and make you want to escape the situation. But could that 'someone' even be you. Are you constantly preoccupied with complaining?

If you're not sure, here are a few markers:

1. Nothing seems like it is good enough.
2. You anticipate something to go wrong.
3. You frequently find fault in how others do things.
4. You generally feel dissatisfied with the way things are.
5. You often express doubt about how something good can happen to you.
6. You say things like: "I doubt it will work." "I didn't think it would..." "I knew I wouldn't..." "Don't tell anyone, but did you know..."
7. You doubt your own decisions.
8. You find optimistic and positive people annoying.
9. You express, "I knew it was going to end up like this!" when something negative happens.

A few years back, there was this employee of mine who seemed to always have something negative to say. He never offered any positive suggestions and instead focused on highlighting the problems. One day, as he continued with his usual negative remarks, I couldn't help but ask him, "Why do you constantly complain about everything? Aren't you happy here? Do you not enjoy your job?" I took the opportunity to explain to him that everyone was working hard to make improvements and create a better working environment and his negative remarks were not helping anyone.

In an instant, his face transformed. It dawned on him right away what he had been doing, and he quickly responded with an apologetic tone, replying "I thought I was just giving suggestions".

He believed he was being helpful, but the issue was that his approach was critical and demoralizing. He swiftly identified problems and areas that needed improvement, yet failed to offer any solutions.

Since then, I've established a principle: if you come across a problem or have something negative to address, it's essential to bring a solution with you.

After that conversation, my employee never complained again. Instead, every time he shared his thoughts on what needed improvement, he provided at least one suggestion that would benefit everyone involved. He would bring a positive solution instead of a complaint.

Criticism is the disapproval of people, not for having faults, but having different faults than yours. Do you complain to your coworkers about your boss or other coworkers? Let me ask you this question, Why are you focusing on them instead of your personal excellence?

All that whining comes with a cost. When we regularly complain and are critical of others, we damage our own body, mind, emotions and deteriorate our future success.

Your negativity breeds toxic relationships and leaves people feeling discouraged. The word "but" has the power to quickly deflate a group discussion and cause discouragement. Consider this scenario: someone suggests an idea, only to be met with a "but..." what comes next is almost always a negative comment.

Any fool can criticize, condemn, and complain, but it takes self-control, discipline, and personal excellence to be positive and optimistic. You see nothing changes when you complain because complaining is a fruitless action.

We hold the power to choose our words and how we speak to others. There is a saying, "Complaining is like bad breath, notice what comes out of someone else's mouth, but not your own". Recognizing and altering this behavior can indeed be challenging.

One of the greatest positive alterations I made in my outlook was when I realized the power of what is often a negative word. I reframed the word "But..." I turn my words from "I have to..." to "I get to..."

With this alteration of the word, instead of saying, "I have to pick up the kids" I say, "I have to pick up the kids, BUT I am so glad I have these amazing kids." In place of uttering, "I have to go to work." I declare, "I need to go to work, BUT I'm so glad I have a job." Instead of, "My boss is all over me about getting this project done." I now pronounce, "...BUT I'm glad my boss trusts me to take on this task." And instead of saying, "I have to clean the house" I express, "BUT, I'm so glad I have a beautiful house to clean".

One of the greatest positive alterations I made in my outlook was when I realized the power of what is often a negative word. I reframed the word "But..." I turn my words from "I have to..." to "I get to..."

With this alteration of the word, instead of saying, "I have to pick up the kids" I say, "I have to pick up the kids, BUT I am so glad I have these amazing kids." In place of uttering, "I have to go to work." I declare, "I need to go to work, BUT I'm so glad I have a job." Instead of, "My boss is all over me about getting this project done." I now pronounce, "...BUT I'm glad my boss trusts me to take on this task." And instead of saying, "I have to clean the house" I express, "BUT, I'm so glad I have a beautiful house to clean".

Complaining can unintentionally turn into a habit that keeps repeating itself. When you engage in repetitive complaining, your brain forms connections between neurons to facilitate the flow of information. This makes it effortless to continue the cycle of complaining in the future. It becomes so effortless that you may not even be aware that you're doing it. In fact, the act of repeatedly complaining reshapes your brain, making it more likely for you to complain in the future. Gradually, without realizing it, you find it easier to focus on the negative rather than the positive, regardless of the circumstances.

Complaining can have a profound negative effect on our mental, emotional, physical, and spiritual well-being. And here's the kicker: complaining actually harms your brain. Studies have revealed that complaining can shrink the hippocampus, which is responsible for emotions and plays a crucial role in problem-solving and intelligent thinking. Moreover, it can also have detrimental effects on your physical health by elevating stress levels and contributing to various physical and psychological ailments.

When you change your perspective, it reduces the stress hormone cortisol by 23%. Research has found that people who cultivate an attitude of gratitude each day experienced improved moods, more energy, substantially less anxiety and successfully achieved more goals.

Most people focus on the problems and are quick to complain to anyone who will listen. These people never get picked to deliver a message to Garcia and then they complain that they never get picked. We have these people in our jobs, homes, churches, community, and schools.

Instead of just focusing on the problem, come to the table with a solution.

If you find yourself having to talk about something or someone in a negative way, try these methods:

1. Before complaining, ask why you are about to discuss it. Are you looking for a solution? Are you looking to make things better? If not, there is a good chance you just want to complain, which is toxic.

2. When you must talk about something negative, start the conversation with something positive, then address the situation, and then end with something positive. Starting and stopping with something positive will help lessen the toxicity of the situation.

3. Be specific. If you must discuss your frustrations, it's not a good time to dredge up every annoyance from the past year. Just address the current situation and be as specific as possible.

Jason R. Doll

Let me clarify something for you. It's important to understand the distinction between complaining and expressing your thoughts or frustrations. Complaining should not be mistaken for informing someone about a mistake or providing guidance on how to avoid repeating it.

As you can see, complaining has absolutely no value. Here's the reality check: when it comes to complaining and being critical, the power to change lies solely within you. No one else can do it for you. It's an internal process. But here's the silver lining: all you need to do is make a simple choice to adjust your attitude.

Rowan accepted that he couldn't control the challenges and environment he would face. Instead, he directed his attention towards what he could control. Rather than dwelling on the uncontrollable, he embraced the controllable aspects of his life.

Don't waste your time complaining, start enjoying life. Don't stress over things beyond your control. Life is a beautiful gift, make the most of it. Choose happiness over complaints.

As an old proverb says, instead of complaining that the rose is full of thorns, be happy that the thorn bush has roses.

Make the most of today because tomorrow is still a mystery to be unraveled.

8,760 Opportunities

I f you live to be 80 years old, which is about the average American life expectancy, then you will experience about 30,000 days or 700,000 hours of life (if we take out sleeping time the number drops to more like 450,000 hours). Broken down further, there are 8,760 hours in a year. In short, there is limited time. How are you using that time?

Since the dawn of human civilization, 'the concept of 'time' has held immense value. Time is limited and can't be stored or transferred. You can't control time. You can't increase it or stop it. It is something that doesn't discriminate against anyone based on age, religion, gender, education, a job title, or how much money you make. Whether you are a billionaire or struggling to make ends meet, time remains constant. Each and every one of us is blessed with the same 24 hours a day, 365 days a year - a total of 8,760 hours annually. However, how we choose to manage and utilize this time differs greatly. Some individuals make the most of their time, while others squander it away.

Time is our most important non-renewable resource. It is far and away the most important commodity in your life. There's a reason why the most successful people agree that time is their most valuable asset: Once it's gone, it's gone forever. Unlike money, you can't earn more time. Once a moment has passed, it belongs to history. The choices we make as individuals about how to spend those 8,760 hours shape our future. How we spend our time matters.

In our fast-paced and demanding world, time is a precious resource that often feels scarce. Each day, we are granted 1,440 minutes to navigate through our personal and professional commitments, pursue our dreams, and find moments of joy and fulfillment. The key lies in understanding how to make the most of these minutes, harnessing their power to boost productivity, achieve goals, and create a balanced and purposeful life.

How do we actually spend our time? We sleep, work, eat, and enjoy leisure time. Across the world, how people spend their time provides an important perspective for understanding what they value most.

Make the most of your time! To achieve our goals, it's crucial that we use our time wisely. Although we're aware of this, we often fail to make the most of the time we have. We frequently find it challenging to determine what truly matters, prioritize effectively, and stay focused on the task at hand amidst distractions, which are bound to happen.

Those individuals who constantly use the excuse of not having enough time to justify their lack of progress and productivity are usually the ones who never reach their full potential. If you claim to have no time, you're simply deceiving yourself. It indicates that you haven't properly prioritized your actions in order to make time for your aspirations and ambitions.

The first thing you need to embrace is that you have the same amount of time as everyone in the world. You have 24 hours a day just like everyone else. So, how are you using it?

Time is not a limited commodity because it is always there, unfolding every second before you.

To unlock the full potential of your time and attain the life you've always envisioned, it's crucial to undergo a mental transformation in your approach to time management. While it's true that we all have a limited number of hours in a day, honing your time management skills can empower you to prioritize what truly counts.

The difference between a person who seems to get everything achieved and a person who never can get things done is how each one chooses to spend their time. Time is just what it is. You do not need more time, nor do you have a lack of time. You can't manage time, it just is. You have all the time before you.

Ah, time management, a term that's thrown around like confetti at a party. It is important to understand that time management is not really a thing. You can't manage time. You can't alter it or adjust it. You can't add to it or pause it. You can't buy it or hold onto it for later. Time is just what it is. You cannot arrange your "time" by making an hour shorter or longer or making time faster or slower.

What you can do is task-management or self-management. What you really manage is your activity during time. "Time management" is a ubiquitous term, it is more accurate to recognize it as "task management."

But what does it really mean? Well, it's all about making the best use of your limited time, my friends. And the key to mastering this art lies in the mystical realm of prioritization.

Task Management means personal productivity skills. It is intentionally taking more control over how you structure and spend your time. Task management is like being the conductor of an orchestra, except instead of musicians, you're directing your own tasks and responsibilities. It's the art of organizing, prioritizing, and completing tasks effectively and efficiently. With so many things constantly vying for our attention, task management helps us stay on track and prevents us from drowning in a sea of unfinished to-dos. Task management plays a crucial role in our productivity.

Over the years, many have asked me, "How do you manage to do everything? Where do you find the time?" Bluntly. It isn't easy. I must sacrifice a lot. I've had to stay up late, get up early, and give up doing certain things in order to achieve the passions and goals I long to achieve.

People say, "I don't have enough time." How many times did you produce this excuse yourself? When people say they "never have enough time", the truth is that they didn't use it wisely. Their vision and passions are not their priority. They have allowed time thieves to suck the marrow out of their lives. To leave time unmanaged is akin to us.

Frankly, we are overwhelmed by text messages, calls, emails, meetings, bills, work challenges, sports, charities, the news, employees, errands, health issues, personal obligations, family responsibilities, among many other things. One of the first things. Ask yourself a straightforward question: "Are the tasks I'm engaging in each day truly valuable and worth my time?"

Consider how you spend your time, particularly your leisure time. Are you making the most of it, or are you simply wasting it away?

Version 1: It's important to recognize that spending two hours watching TV, scrolling through social media, playing golf, or simply doing nothing significant every day means we're not fully dedicating ourselves to our goals. We've all been guilty of wasting time on things that don't truly matter or align with our dreams and ambitions.

Don't get me wrong, I love having some downtime to relax and watch movies. It's important to take time for yourself and enjoy activities like watching TV, using social media, playing sports, or simply doing nothing. However, it's worth considering if we're spending too much time on these activities. Is it possible to cut back a few hours and use that time to focus on personal growth?

Ask yourself if you are filling your free time with activities to merely eliminate boredom or if you are using your time to be effective to reach your full potential. What most people misunderstand is that being busy doesn't mean you're being productive. I used to confuse being busy with being successful and productive. It is not the same. You can be very busy, without living out your priorities or moving closer to your goals. It's a frustrating and disappointing place to be.

Many individuals waste their time on unimportant tasks that lead them nowhere. Consequently, when they fail to accomplish their goals, they often attribute it to their busy schedules and life itself. However, is a shortage of time truly the underlying cause?

> There's a big difference between a workaholic verses a high performer.

Absolutely not! The reality is, the concept of not having time simply doesn't exist. It all boils down to how effectively you manage and juggle your time. The primary reason why people feel they don't have enough time is because they have an overwhelming number of responsibilities to handle. According to a recent study, 41% of adults in the United States admitted to not having sufficient time in a day to accomplish all their planned tasks.

It's a fact that a lot of us have busy schedules and responsibilities that consume our time. However, the way we decide to utilize that time, including our leisure time, greatly impacts our overall satisfaction. Many individuals struggle with managing their personal time effectively. Although many believe they can, the truth is that if they truly could, they would be able to find a harmonious balance and lead a more fulfilling life.

In the workplace, there is a widespread epidemic. Managers are constantly using phrases that are being adopted by their employees as a form of pride. They often say things like, "I'm incredibly swamped." "I pulled a 16-hour shift." "I didn't even take a break over the weekend." And the list goes on. It's undeniable that our leaders have numerous responsibilities that keep them busy and overwhelmed. However, the issue lies in the fact that everyone is busy. The problem with these statements is that we fail to recognize the true worth of our work and the importance of effectively managing our time.

This isn't just in the workforce; I've seen it in people's personal lives. I've seen it for my own. One day, I realized I was being "productive" for the sake of being productive. Many of us are wearing "doing productivity" as a status symbol. We enjoy the feeling when people describe us as "productive." For me, after a while of "doing" productivity, I feel I can no longer keep up. I eventually crashed and burned. I realized that I was not really going anywhere. I had to stop *doing* and had to start *being* productive.

We all want to do more with what we have. Unfortunately, we think being busy means we are making strides. There's a big difference between a workaholic versus a high performer. You can work hard and achieve very little.

The good news is that personal time productivity skills is an ability you can easily master. Balance is the most important thing in your life and unless you start taking control of how you utilize your time, you will always be stressed and struggling to reach your purpose. People who continue their life without proper balance reach their saturation point faster and this is where everything starts to fall apart.

There's no one personal productivity skills management system or strategies that will work for everyone. Here are some principles that are vital to understand.

1. You can't *manage* time. The only thing you can manage is the way you use time.
2. The success of any task/time management strategies you use will be determined by your personal motivation to succeed.
3. You will never be able to do everything that everyone you interact with wants you to do.
4. People who successfully manage their use of time do so by prioritizing their activities so they can obtain their goals.

To achieve your goals and ambitions, to fulfill your mission, it is crucial to take control. You need to be the one running the day, rather than letting it run you. Some individuals will excel at managing their time, while others will find themselves being controlled by it. It is essential to ensure that you become the master of your time. The first step is to identify where your time is being spent and determine your top priorities. This will lead you to the fundamental task of prioritizing and managing competing priorities. Once you have a clear understanding of your goals, priorities, and values, you can assess how you are utilizing your time. Are you putting first things first? Putting first things first means focusing on the most important aspects of life. To truly master your time, you must first be aware of your priorities.

If you don't get your priorities in order, it just shows you don't want this bad enough, maybe you're just all talk. Those are tough words, but it should be one that drives you to get up and not allow anything to keep you from dashing forward.

1. Align your actions. Get clear on what you want and align your needs to get there with your actions.
2. Prioritize. You can't direct your energy to your goals if you don't know what you want your results to be.
3. Zero in. Better time usage skills start with zeroing in on your core values.
4. Don't get in the weeds. Make decision on what actually needs your time or what could be schedule for later, or not at all (See below)
5. Don't meet to meet. Don't have or participate in meetings that have no value. If you can't identify what you want to leave with, ask if it is worth your time.
6. Set Smart Goals. Be clear about the outcome you plan to achieve. SMART goals are Specific, Measurable, Achievable, Realistic, and anchored within a Time Frame.
7. Don't multitask. multitasking is taxing on the brain, overloading its working memory, and badly hurts productivity.
8. Say "No". You can't focus your energy on the proper places if you can't say, "No".

President Eisenhower used a matrix to help him make the best choices. He had it broken down into four categories. Consider breaking your tasks down like his:

1. Do first. Things that are urgent and important which need your attention.
2. Schedule. These are items that are less urgent but important which can be addressed at a later time.
3. Delegate. Items which need attention but can be addressed by another person.
4. Don't do. These items are neither urgent nor important.

To attain personal excellence, you must make sure you spend your time focused on the real priorities. Your time is limited.

Luckily, several prioritization techniques can come to our rescue. The ABC method, where tasks are classified as A (high priority), B (medium priority), or C (low priority), helps us focus on what really matters. The Eisenhower Matrix, with its four quadrants separating tasks into urgent, important, not urgent, and not important, helps us identify tasks worth our time and attention. These techniques provide valuable frameworks to ensure we're not just busy bees buzzing around not really achieving much, but rather that we are productive superheroes saving the day.

Mastering the art of task management is crucial for optimizing productivity and achieving success. By understanding the importance of task management, focusing on essential elements, implementing effective strategies for prioritization, utilizing appropriate tools and techniques, and overcoming common challenges, individuals and teams can streamline their workflows and accomplish more in less time.

There are 1,440 minutes in a day. That means we have 1,440 daily opportunities to make a positive impact. Use your time wisely.

To incorporate the "Message to Garcia" philosophy into our lives, we can start by adopting a proactive mindset. Taking initiative, embracing challenges, and being resourceful are key aspects of this philosophy.

The message portrayed in "A Message to Garcia" remains highly relevant in today's fast-paced world. The ability to take initiative, overcome challenges, communicate effectively, and lead by example continues to be valued and sought after in both personal and professional settings.

Excellence is not

an act

but a Habit.

– Jason R. Doll

Traits of Victorious People

THE PURSUIT OF EXCELLENCE

W e all have our own definition of success. Whether it's achieving a personal goal, overcoming a challenge, or reaching a milestone, victory often signifies success and accomplishment.

But what sets victorious people apart from the rest? What traits do they possess that allow them to conquer challenges and emerge triumphant? In this article, we will explore the key traits of victorious people and discover how we can incorporate these characteristics into our own lives.

Success comes in various ways and forms, although, when you examine successful people, there are common traits among them.

Over the years, I have seen similar traits first-hand in a diverse set of successful people I've worked with and known over the years. From great leaders, billionaires, CEOs, Olympians, astronauts, to successful entrepreneurs, they have all demonstrated similar characters. Each one was different and yet they all shared much of the same DNA when it came to the traits that made them successful.

Some people want to be successful leaders, yet they look for the smoothest road to their goal. Ideally, they want a contain with instructions that direct them to add scoop two tablespoons of magic formula in with a glass of water, mix and drink – and they will be great leaders. The problem is, there is no drink. There is no magic formula, it is a choice and mindset to be the best version of themselves.

Victorious people possess a unique set of traits that propel them towards success. It is only through striving for excellence that we can discover our full potential.

Here are 25 effective habits of successful people. Learn them, implement them, live them, and make them your own.

1. *Passion* - People who experience success don't only have passion; they live with it. Passion is key to success!

2. *Purpose and Vision* - Successful people have a clear and defined purpose for their life.

3. *Goal-Orientation* - They are habitual goal setters who dedicate themselves daily to working on their objectives.

4. *Excellence* - No matter what, successful people pursue excellence. They become the best in their field.

5. *Perseverance* - Extraordinary people are determined and persistent. They don't allow circumstances to deter them from their goals and dreams.

6. *Positive Attitude* - A positive attitude allows them to persevere no matter what they are facing.

7. *Exceed Expectations* - Do the difficult tasks others avoid. The person who repeatedly gets things done is the one who will be called on for the important responsibilities. By doing tough jobs with excellence, you develop a reputation and are called upon for the important tasks.

8. *Speak Positively and Successfully* - Your worlds have power. They bread life. What you say is what you will reproduce.

9. *Big Thinker, Big Dreamer* - I have yet to meet a successful person who didn't have extraordinary dreams. When you think big, you act big, and big things happen. If you want to know whether someone will be successful, ask them about their dreams.

10. *Focus* - People who achieve greatness know how to work through all that distraction. They don't take their eyes off the prize.

11. *Integrity* - This is the most important attribute you can possess. An attitude of integrity and honesty is critical. Integrity is the essence of all things.

12. *Communicators* - Strong communication is essential for success. People who can communicate effectively excel in life. Good communication skills are key.

13. *Action Orientation* - Successful people are doers, not talkers. They don't wait for conditions to be perfect before they act.

14. *Optimism* - People who achieve excellence are optimistic. They don't dwell on the "what if's" but focus on the goal. What others can't see, they can! They expect to be successful in their endeavors.

15. *Self-confidence* - People of great achievement trust and believe in themselves. People with ambition have display a healthy level of confidence.

16. *Risk Takers* - Those who achieve victory are risk takers. They know you can't make important gains without taking important risks. They have the courage to begin and continue all the way through. They are "all in."

17. *Listeners* – People love speaking, but those who succeed in life strive to be excellent listeners. People who succeed in life listen and ask questions.

18. *Preparedness* – Extraordinary people are always prepared. They are prepared to act, even when someone approaches unexpectedly and asks them to find Garcia. They also not only have a Plan B but also a Plan C, D, E, and F.

19. *Willpower* – One cannot achieve excellence without the strength to see things through. When you want it, you will make it happen.

20. *Know to say "no"* – Those who are successful can say "no." Sometimes we must say "no" so that we can say "yes" to what is most important.

21. *Improvement* –Successful people never stop improving themselves. They are always learning and growing.

22. *Givers* – Successful people are generous givers and love to help others. They make it a habit to bring value to others. They look for opportunities to direct, encourage, and motivate others.

23. *Vision* – Victorious people have vision. They think about and plan for the future with imagination and wisdom. They are not short sighted.

24. *Self-Control* – Successful people don't panic. They control their emotions. They understand that they can't always change what's happening, but they know they have control over how they respond to it.

25. *Commitment* - Successful people have unswerving commitment. They follow through, doing whatever it takes to make it happen.

As you read through these, what traits did you realize that you already possess, and which do you need to adopt?

The traits of victorious individuals provide a roadmap for success and personal growth. Cultivating these traits requires dedication, effort, and a commitment to personal development. By embodying the traits of victorious people, we can navigate challenges, overcome obstacles, and create a fulfilling and successful life journey.

By cultivating these habits, you can enhance your productivity, achieve your aspirations, and transform your life. It is important to consistently work on improving these habits throughout your lifetime. Although it may not be effortless, the ultimate reward will be significant, benefiting both your personal and professional growth.

A positive mindset plays a crucial role in achieving victory. It helps individuals stay focused, motivated, and optimistic, even in the face of challenges. By maintaining a positive outlook, individuals can overcome obstacles more effectively, find creative solutions, and attract supportive and like-minded individuals, all of which contribute to their overall success.

Yes, anyone has the potential to become a victorious person. While certain traits may come more naturally to some individuals, these qualities can be developed and cultivated through practice, determination, and self-reflection. It is important to remember that becoming a victorious person is a journey, and each individual's path to success may vary.

To become a victorious individual, it takes more than luck or talent. It requires cultivating key traits that set you apart from the crowd. So, whether you're chasing victory in your career, relationships, or personal goals, remember to nurture these traits. You'll be well on your way to becoming a true champion. Now, go forth and conquer!

Your ability to succeed in any endeavor boils down to this question: can you carry a message to Garcia?

If you are going to achieve

excellence in the big things,

you must first develop habits of
excellence in the little things.

– Jason R. Doll

Self–Reflection

THE PURSUIT OF EXCELLENCE

Now that we have all the essential tools at our disposal, it's time to delve deep into it and gain a clear understanding of our current life situation and future aspirations. Grab a pen and get ready to jot down your thoughts. To begin, let's stimulate our minds by answering the following questions.

Do you have the spark of what it takes to be a person of excellence? Do you have what it takes to deliver a message to Garcia?

Excellence is an enduring journey of self–discovery and blinding detours. Where are you excelling at living a life with excellence? Where are you strong at and where do you need to improve? This is a time for self–reflection.

Learning about yourself takes a lot of time, but it's well worth the investment. The more you know about yourself, the better decisions you'll make about the lifestyle you've always wanted to live.

Self-reflection means taking the time to look more deeply into yourself—and at the external forces that are shaping your life. Today is the day to begin to see and establish personal excellence as your standard in all things.

Get started now: Self-evaluation questions:

1. What does personal excellence mean to you?
2. What has stopped you from applying the ideas of personal excellence in the past?
3. What is preventing you today from pushing past the status quo?

Self-Assessment

Fill in the following self–assessment.
Yes or **No**

Do you have a mindset of personal excellence?	
Are you living with passion and purpose?	
Do you always give your personal best?	
Are you working to achieve your goals and purpose in life?	
Are you doing all you can to achieve your passion and purpose?	
Are you living an intentional life?	
Do you give up when things are tough?	
Do you display a positive attitude?	
Are you willing to improve your attitude?	
Are you willing to increase your level of excellence?	
Are you using my time wisely?	
Do you have a sense of purpose and direction in life?	
Do you take responsibility for your actions?	
Do you give value to the world?	
Would you be known as a person of excellence?	
Do you desire more in life?	
Do you long to hear your name as someone who is like Rowan?	
Do you want others to know you are a person who can be trusted with important tasks on an important mission?	

Self-Assessment

Fill in the following self–assessment.

A = Strong
B = Above Average
C = Average habit
D = Below Average

Positive and Constructive Attitude	
Do you display Personal Excellence	
Desire for Excellence	
Willingness to Give Your Best	
Willingness to Change	
Willingness to Look for Opportunities to Excel	
Willingness to Improve Performance	
Willingness to Improve Character	
Willingness to Improve Attitude	
Willingness to Accept Positive Feedback	
Willingness to Get Out of Your Comfort Zone	
Willingness to Take Risks	
Willingness to Do More Than Others	
Level of Commitment	
Do you Speaks Positively	
Your Integrity	
Do you Rarely Complains or Criticizes	
Do you set Goals	
Encouragement of Self	
Encouragement of Others	
Confidence Level	
Tendency to Smile	

A person who can

carry a message
to Garcia

are a special breed of people.

They are the ones who

change the world.

- Jason R. Doll

Self-Assessment

EXCELLENCE *AT EVERY LEVEL*

Write down you answers for the following questions:

What does *'personal excellence'* mean to you? _____

_____

_____

_____

_____

What is your purpose and direction in life? _____

_____

_____

_____

_____

What is your passion that drives you? _____

_____

_____

_____

_____

What defines you? _____

_____

_____

_____

_____

_____

_____

_____

What drives me to excel? _____

_____

_____

_____

_____

How do you want to be remembered in your obituary?

_____

_____

_____

_____

Are you dedicated to excellence? If so, how do you display it?

_____

_____

_____

_____

_____

What are your core values? _____

_____

_____

_____

_____

What areas do you need to grow in? Why? What will you go
about it? _____

_____

_____

_____

_____

What motivates you? _____

_____

_____

_____

_____

How do you best express a positive attitude? _____

_____

_____

_____

Are you dependable? How have you demonstrated it? _____

_____

_____

_____

_____

What is your life's purpose? Write a mission statement.

_____

_____

_____

_____

_____

_____

_____

What are your strengths? _____

_____

_____

_____

What restores you? _____

_____

_____

_____

What makes you stand out as a person of excellence? _____

_____

_____

_____

_____

_____

_____

_____

How can you do to improve the level of excellence in all you do? _____

_____

_____

What can you do to inspire other people? _____

_____

_____

_____

What positive habits do you need to develop? _____

_____

_____

_____

_____

What are your top priorities? _____

_____

_____

_____

_____

_____

_____

_____

What do you need to do differently in your life to be a person of excellence? How can you be more like Lt. Rowan?

_____

_____

_____

_____

_____

_____

_____

_____

List the core areas of your life where you want to get results.

_____

_____

_____

_____

_____

_____

_____

_____

What do you think you can apply to your life from the story "A Message to Garcia"?

_____

_____

_____

_____

_____

_____

_____

_____

What qualities need your attention? What will you do to instill those in your life?

_____

_____

_____

_____

_____

_____

_____

_____

Lt. Andrew Rowan

Andrew S. Rowan (April 23, 1857 – January 10, 1943) was born in Gap Mills, West Virginia.

Rowan enrolled in the United States Military Academy at West Point in 1877 at the age of twenty and was commissioned second lieutenant in 1881.

At the outbreak of the Spanish–American campaign, a disguised Lieutenant Rowan, crossed the enemy lines in the province of Oriente (the eastern part of Cuba), traversed the nation, and succeeded in delivering a message to General Calixto García of the Cuban rebels. On the same journey, he also discovered and reported on clandestine Spanish military conditions in that region. His information contributed to the quick victory of the U.S. Army and end to the war.

The Distinguished Service Cross was presented to Andrew S. Rowan, Captain, U.S. Army, for extraordinary heroism in action in connection with the operations in Cuba in May 1898.

ELBERT HUBBARD

THE PURSUIT OF EXCELLENCE

Elbert Green Hubbard (June 19, 1856 – May 7, 1915) was an American writer, publisher, and philosopher.

Hubbard was born in the city of Bloomington, Illinois.

He wrote the story recounted in this book, "A Message to Garcia."

ABOUT THE AUTHOR

THE PURSUIT OF EXCELLENCE

Jason Doll is a speaker, author, pastor, and businessman who is enthusiastic about inspiring others. His books have included award-winning publications. Jason's inspirational and charismatic communication style inspires others to positively change their lives.

A former police chief, public safety director and CEO, Jason is now devoted to helping others around the world progress in their spiritual, family, and professional life. With his pastor's heart, Jason longs to comfort the brokenhearted and to heal the hurting. He started a global ministry to serve others in different countries.

Jason adores his family and has loved raising his four wonderful children. Together, they have fun making memories and finding new adventures.

Over the years, Jason has had numerous opportunities to share his testimony and life-changing messages worldwide. Working in different countries, Jason started a worldwide ministry to help encourage, motivate, and serve others.

Ultimately, Jason shares his testimony and the life-changing message of the Gospel worldwide.

REFERENCES

Hubbard, Elbert. "A Message to Garcia." *The Philistine*, March 1899.

Rowan, Andrew Summers. "How I Carried the Message to Garcia." San Francisco: William D. Harney, 1922.